SCIENCE EDUCATION PROGRAMME IN SECONDARY SCHOOLS

Science Education Programme in Secondary Schools

RAJASHREE MOHANTY

DEEP & DEEP PUBLICATIONS PVT. LTD.
F-159, Rajouri Garden, New Delhi - 110027

SCIENCE EDUCATION PROGRAMME
IN SECONDARY SCHOOLS

ISBN 81-7629-552-3

Typeset by THE COMPOSERS,
260 C.A. Apt., Paschim Vihar, New Delhi - 110 063

Printed in India at ELEGANT PRINTERS,
A 38/2, Phase-I, Mayapuri, New Delhi - 110 064

Published by DEEP & DEEP PUBLICATIONS PVT. LTD.,
F-159, Rajouri Garden, New Delhi-110 027
Phones : 25435369, 25440916.

E-mail: ddpbooks@yahoo.co.in • deep98@del13.vsnl.net.in
Showroom:
2/13, Ansari Road, Daryaganj, New Delhi-110002 • Telefax: 23245122

Contents

Preface

This is the age of Science and Technology and it has been witnessing a lot of changes in our life and environment. Science has left its impact in every walk of our life. Through Science education we can make our students knowledgeable and interested in various aspects of Science and Technology. We can inculcate Scientific spirit and temper and develop Scientific aptitude among students at all levels. However, there are many problems in the field of science education and we can bring about improvement in the quality of Science teaching by identifying the problems and addressing them effectively.

In this book attempts have been made to present the national scenario of Science Education and show its importance in school curriculum. Hence, historical as well as philosophical perspectives of Science education have been discussed. Besides theoretical discussions, the writer has taken the views and suggestions of the people at the helm of the affairs as well as working in the actual class rooms. It is therefore felt that this book is useful from practical points of view in various aspects.

I express my gratitude to my esteemed Teacher Dr. Subhash Chandra Panda, Reader in Education, RIE, Bhubaneswar, my father Prof. Jagannath Mohanty and Dr. S.K. Choudhury for their academic assistance and support.

I am also highly indebted to, Smt. A. Mohanty, Miss S. Mohanty, Dr. T. Das, Smt. S. Choudhury for their substantial help. I offer my sincere thanks to the esteemed experts, heads of institutions visited, librarians of different libraries for their helping hand in supplying relevant data and related literature pertaining to the book.

I extend my sincere gratitude to Mr. Haraprasad Mohanty for providing computer facility and Mr. Pradeep Kumar Swain for printing of the book.

Last but not the least, I must express my thanks to M/s. Deep and Deep Publications Private Limited, New Delhi, for undertaking publication of this book.

Bhubaneswar RAJASHREE MOHANTY

1

Science Education

1.1 INTRODUCTION

Science has brought about revolutionary changes in every walk of our life. Its impact is visible everywhere and in every aspect of our existence, i.e. vocational, social, economic, political and cultural. We solely depend on science for domestic amenities, industrial productions, communication, defence, medicine, agriculture, transport and so many other matters. So, in each and every country special attention is given for the development of science.

Science, therefore, occupies a very important place in curriculum both at school and university stages of education in India. It becomes a priority area in education, both at the compulsory education level as well as the level of specialisation. Science education is supposed to perform a two-fold task. Firstly, in individual perspective, the cultivation of a scientific temper, spirit of enquiry, disposition to reason logically, habit of judging beliefs and formation of opinions based on available evidence, readiness to reject unfounded theories and principles have been emphasized in science education. And secondly, in the social perspective, science education has aimed at equipping individuals to participate in the creation of a society which is free from poverty, hunger, diseases and evils such as violence, exploitation, oppression, etc.

Various Education Commissions and Committees have been appointed by our National Government after Independence. All of them have recommended for modernizing the system of science teaching in our education system at every level. There has been significant improvement in science teaching in India after 1970, as compared to that of the pre-Independence period.

There has been 10 + 2 + 3 system of education at the national level, where maximum importance has been given to science education. Thus throughout India, the whole curriculum in science has undergone change with the broader objectives of providing every student with adequate knowledge, about the physical and biological world around him/her in order to enable him/her to take intelligent decisions and for attacking and solving personal as well as environmental problems.

1.2 NATURE OF SCIENCE EDUCATION IN INDIA

Most of the changes of our country have been effected by science and technology. In reality, science, more than any other subject in the traditional school curriculum, has been closely associated with economic and social development of our society. Science Education offers a knowledge base and a way of knowing which can be 'applied' for effective solution of human environmental problems and to industrial development. Science Education enlightens the young generation in the following areas of knowledge:

- Knowledge of science for healthy living-personal as well as social.
- Knowledge of science for agriculture.
- Knowledge of science for ecological balance.
- Knowledge of science for nutrition.
- Knowledge of science for clean environment and its protection.
- Knowledge of science for job requirement.

Science Education in schools prepares pupils to deal with the innumerable problems of life with a scientific attitude. Including science, as one of the subjects in the school curriculum is not enough. Maximising the achievement of pupils in science is the main concern of science education.

The primary task in science education must include the transaction of activities which need be simple, clear and unequivocal, so as eliminate doubt, uncertainty, and difficulty. Secondly, it conducts test which aims at discovering what the students actually know and how far they are capable of applying the knowledge in their lives and activities.

The failure in examinations and low achievement in science is very much baffling. Many studies revealed that factors such as intelligence, attitude, socio-economic status, study habits and other correlates of the school are the non-intellectual factors which affect achievement. There is significant difference in the achievement of pupils in science studying in rural and urban schools. Pupils in urban areas scored more in science than those in rural areas (Rup Prakash, 1968).

The Education Commission of 1964-66 remarks, "If science is poorly taught and badly learnt, it is little more than burdening the mind with dead information and it could degenerate into a new superstition. What we need is improvement in the standard and quality of science education at all levels in the country". Better science education naturally demands better facilities for providing it. The essential provisions needed for effective science education are:

(a) An upto-date dynamic science syllabus.
(b) A properly qualified willing teacher who loves the subject and the learners.
(c) Essential science material and equipment.
(d) A well-equipped laboratory.
(e) Rich library.
(f) A programme of co-curricular and extra-curricular activities to supplement the class room teaching.

The development and prosperity of any country depends now on the ability of that country to utilize the upto-date knowledge of technology. The developing countries like India are depending on advanced countries for technical assistance. But no country having self-respect can afford to rely on this type of foreign assistance for a long time. Hence, India has to build up a sound system of science education at all levels.

By virtue of the scientific method or the systematic process, science can only be an instrument in solving present and future human problems. It is the man, who actually solves his own problems by the help of science. So it is necessary for them to know what the scientists do so as to make one familiar with the scientific facts and principles. In view of this, a sound system of science education, from the lowest level of schooling becomes imperative. It has therefore, been included in the Elementary as well as Secondary stages of education, but its quality has to be improved at all costs.

Every individual in a democracy like India must be benefited by the knowledge of science for various considerations. Some such points are enumerated below:

- Science education can assist the individual in making adjustments to new conditions arising from the faster moving scientific advancement and discovery.
- Science education can develop the rational thought process in the citizens which would lead to a better social order.
- The laws of science form the basis of universal understanding irrespective of language, colour and religion.
- Science education can offer the individual an introduction to the broad area of physical and biological phenomena and many other aesthetic features as well as sense of appreciation.

On account of the multifarious values of science and its contribution to development of scientific attitude and scientific method, science commands a special position in the world of human knowledge and learning. It is therefore very much appropriate to provide and improve science education in all spheres of the country.

Government of India in the National Policy on Education (NPE, 1986, p. 23) makes the following statements on Science Education under Re-orienting the Content and Process of Education:

- Science education will be strengthened so as to develop in the child well-defined abilities and values, such as the spirit of enquiry, creativity, objectivity, the courage to question and an aesthetic sensibility.
- Science education programme will be designed to enable the learner to acquire problem-solving and decision-making skills and to discover the relationship of science with health, agriculture, industry and other aspects of daily life. Every effort will be made to internalise science education to the vast numbers who have remained outside the pale of formal education.

In searching to understand the meaning of science education, it is found essential to identify the characteristics of teachers that might make a difference in student outcomes. The process-product description of teaching methods have an impact on the classroom climate and ultimately on how much students learn. Research in science education has focussed on three sets of variables: the instructional system, the teacher and the student. Current researches in science education reveal much about students and their characteristics that appear to influence classroom interactions and the outcomes of science learning. The researches on science education focussed more on studying the characteristics of students as they are related to successful achievement and development of positive attitudes towards science.

Pioneering researches have been conducted in science education to give a synoptic view of the trends and highlighted the major aspects of science education.

1.2.1 Major Aspects of Science Education to be Strengthened

In view of improving the standard of science education in secondary schools, several steps and programmes have been launched to strengthen different aspects of science education. These are stated below:

1.2.1.1 Curriculum for Science Teaching

The Education Commission (1964-66) has recommended that Science and Mathematics should be taught on a compulsory basis to all pupils as a part of general education during the first ten years of schooling. In addition, there should be provision of special courses in these subjects at the secondary stage for students of more than average ability.

Conceptually Oriented Programme in Elementary Science (COPES) project was started in 1969 under the sponsorship of New York University and supported by the U.S.A Office of Education. The COPES curriculum is action centered. Almost all activities require exploration of non-reading nature to be carried out by the individual or small groups of students. It is also a fundamental principle of COPES that the major and supporting science concepts are being developed within the structured sequences, basic skills, where appropriate teaching materials must be concurrently developed and refined.

The Report of the Review Committee (1977) as quoted by Sharma (1988) on the curriculum for the ten years school has recommended curriculum for the first ten years of school education with equal importance on Language, Mathematics, Science, Social Studies, Social Useful Productive Work, Games and Creative Activities such as Music, Dancing and Painting.

1.2.1.2 Teacher to Teach Science

The Government of India, UNESCO and UNICEF entered into an agreement in 1967 for reorganising and strengthening teaching of science throughout the school stage. Preparation of new syllabus and instructional materials, text books, teachers' guides and laboratory materials and steps to improve the teacher training programmes were given utmost importance.

In 1969, UNESCO sent an exploratory mission to Thailand to determine possibility of developing a national science teaching centre. Its report contained suggestions to the government of Thailand for action in preparing request for financial and technical assistance from United Nations Development Programme (UNDP) and UNESCO. As a result in 1972 the Thai government established in Bangkok a large curriculum project under the joint sponsorship of UNESCO/UNDP and was given the name as Institute for Promotion of Teaching Science and Technology (IPTST) (Sharma, 1988). As teachers occupy a key position in education, importance on qualification of teacher, adequate training, etc. were emphasised.

1.2.1.3 Laboratory to Perform Science Activities

While suggesting the plan for the science laboratory, panel for Science education in secondary schools kept in view the recommendations of the 'Report on Science Teaching in Schools' by UNESCO Planning Mission of Experts, the plan has accepted on principles that because of limited financial resources of our country it will be economical and beneficial to provide combined Lecture-hall-*cum*-Laboratory in High Schools to facilitate the science teaching-learning in secondary schools.

1.2.1.4 Methods of Teaching and Teaching Aids used in Teaching Science

Methods of teaching have undergone change a lot in its approach to make the subject simple and lucid. The traditional teacher centered approaches changed to pupil centered indifferent ways. Some of these are Heuristic method, Assignment method, Project method, Discussion method, Problem solving method, etc. Use of aids gives living touch to teach a subject. The traditional aids become redundant in the modern time with the advent of audio-visual aids. The two-dimensional and three-dimensional aids, projected and non-projected aids and sophisticated aids like television, computer, etc are to be utilized in class room situation to make the science teaching more lively in addition to localized low-cost and no-cost aids.

1.3 IMPORTANCE OF SCIENCE EDUCATION IN SCHOOL CURRICULUM

A few decades back, science was not popular among common people. It was limited to certain class of people. Now, science has established its claim to be placed in the school curriculum. It has now been recognised as a compulsory subject from the beginning of school education. There is now rapid change and advance in science and technology and the growing complexity of industrial and economic organisation. There is increasing demand for larger number of highly skilled and trained personnel drawn from different disciplines and functioning generally in composite teams, rather than as individuals. Science becomes a part and parcel of our life. Hence, from the beginning of education more stress is to be given on science education to meet the growing demands of the society.

Science is a very useful subject in the school and the range of this usefulness extends from simple problems in daily life to complex problems in the various branches of higher scientific studies. We are living in an age of science and technology. If our country is to keep in step with rapidly changing world:

- Firstly, our school must be able to prepare students who can master efficiently the latest developments in all fields of science and technology are being discovered every year.

- Secondly, our school curriculum should adhere scientific values to enhance the pragmatic attitude among the pupil.
- Thirdly, secondary school is an appropriate stage for the initiation of the future scientists, it is essential that the teaching of science must have a prominent place in the secondary schools of our country.

According to Kothari Commission report (1966), at the secondary level, science as a discipline of the mind and a preparation for higher education deserves special emphasis. In the lower secondary classes, Physics, Chemistry, Biology and Earth Science should be taught as compulsory subjects for all the pupils. Building on the introductory courses at the earlier stages, they should cover wider areas and go deeper into the content than before. The changing character of the sciences should be the major factor in curriculum development.

National Policy on Education (1986) has taken science as one of the subjects in the core-curriculum for ten-year schooling. Thus, children need to possess considerable knowledge of science to understand its influence on human affairs. Some of the reasons to include science as a school subject are follows:

- In this 'Science-technology-oriented' society every citizen should be able to understand the role of science in agriculture, food, health, energy, industry, environment and ecological concerns. It is evident that proper development in science can only occur if citizens are informed and are able to contribute to the making of decisions involving science-based issues.
- The understanding of science and technology needs decisions making ability about personal hygiene, nutrition, safety, disposal of waste products, control of pollution and the industrial hazards.
- Understanding the importance of science for society, in relation to economic, industrial and social aspects.
- Science satisfies the curiosity of learners through its ever increasing sphere of knowledge and innovations.
- Science has a direct bearing on the social aspect which is related to living including ethical, social and moral aspects of life.

- Science has its own values such as objectivity and rationality. Its application in agriculture, industry and allied fields has increased the productivity of the nation.

The Revised National Policy on Education (1992) has observed that there is erosion of essential values and the increasing dynamism in society has brought to focus the need for readjustments in curriculum in order to make education a forceful tool for the cultivation of social and moral values. Education as an organised social system has an important function in the development of moral, spiritual and aesthetic values. In science class rooms too a science teacher can not avoid dealing with values. The values are to be inculcated among the students through science education effectively so as to make them a true citizen of the nation.

1.3.1 Science Curriculum Policy

Science curriculum policy-making is an area of Science Education that has began to receive the attention of researchers only recently. Science curriculum policies are official legally binding statements what counts as science education. Virtually every educational jurisdiction in the world has its ways of making science curriculum policy known to its schools.

According to Programme of Action of the Revised National Policy on Education (1992), the aims of teaching science at this stage is primarily directed towards problem-solving and decision-making through the learning of key concepts which cut across all the disciplines of science. The content of science and the learning ability of the pupils should reflect that science is a continuing human endeavour and it is international in character and method.

The instructional materials based on the framework will be reviewed to ensure that the approaches followed are in consonance with the objectives of science education as laid down in the policy to develop in the child well defined abilities and values such as spirit of enquiry, creativity, objectivity, courage to question and aesthetic sensibility, learning of science will be oriented to ensure that the learners discover the relationship of science with health, agriculture, industry and other aspects of daily life.

1.3.2 Changing Nature of Science Curriculum

In India efforts have been made to develop indigenous science curriculum, new science text books, to revitalize science teaching. The National curriculum for Primary and Secondary Education: A Framework, 1985 developed by NCERT has highlighted the need for core-curriculum where science will be an integral part from Class-I to Class-X. Science will be started as environmental studies at the primary stage. The main thrust is towards the realization of developmental and integrative aspects of education. One of the important aspect of curriculum is the organizational aspect which necessitates effective integration, adequate balance and proper relevance. Since text books are the extension form of curriculum, these three aspects should be given proper attention, perhaps the most important thing is to link theory and practice. This depends mostly on the Boards of School Education where curriculum is developed and science teachers who put it to action in the classroom.

In the National Curriculum for Primary and Secondary Education: A Framework, 1985 the NCERT has mentioned that Science Education should develop well defined abilities in cognitive and affective domains and also psycho-motor skills. It should help in the development of certain abilities and values such as spirit of enquiry, creativity, objectivity, courage to question and aesthetic sensitivity. These expectations need new directions in science teaching.

1.3.3 School Improvement Programmes Through Curriculum Development in Science

During the last ten years a great expansion has taken place as regards to the increase in the number of institutions and the number of children going to schools. But proportionately there has not been much change in the curriculum.

The NCERT has been working towards the improvement of the quality of instruction in schools. In order to achieve this goal, the various departments of the National Institute of Education (NIE) and NCERT have been working for revision of curriculum and production of model text books and other instructional materials. The work on these aspects has been organised at various levels of school stage and in different subjects. The Department of Curriculum and Evaluation of the NIE is finalising the subject syllabi and preparing a comprehensive curriculum plan for the entire school stage.

Similarly, the Department of Education in Science and Mathematics (DESM) of the NIE is preparing prototypes of new science equipment with indigenous materials. The Board of Secondary Education (BSE) and State Council of Educational Research and Training (SCERT) have been entrusted with the responsibility of development of curriculum and instructional materials. Improvement of Science Education programme in secondary school is an important task before the organisation which is to be done on priority basis. It is a well known fact that there has been an explosion in the knowledge of science, its techniques and methodologies. For full utilisation of the possibilities of science for economic development and betterment of life, it is necessary that new competencies may be developed among the future citizens. For this purpose it is imperative that a new and dynamic curriculum in science may replace the present outmoded curriculum. Quality instructional materials in science including text-books may be developed. The DESM of the NIE is working towards this end at national level.

There is an awakening now that the teachers (who are actually to teach the syllabus) should be involved in the revision of the curriculum. Quality of education also depends on such programmes as improvements of curriculum and text-books, adoption of modern methods of teaching and evaluation. The following programmes can be taken up to improve science teaching at the secondary level.

(A) Revision of Science Curricula at Different Levels

A major objective of this programme should be to orient education to national needs. This would include programmes such as promoting national consciousness, emphasising character formation through cultivation of moral, social and spiritual values, improving science education, introducing work experience and national or social service stressing physical education, games and sports and developing a rich and varied plans of co-curricular activities.

At the school stage, there is an urgent need to upgrade and improve science curricula at different levels to increase pupil's knowledge in content and to provide scope adequately for the development of life skills and inculcation of right interests, attitudes and values.

(B) Adoption of Improved Methods of Teaching and Evaluation

This programme should be promoted through research, improved supervision, in-service training of teachers, production of literature and establishment of science teachers' association.

(C) Book Development Programmes

These will include the following:

(i) The production of text books in English and Modern Indian languages which contain Indian experience. Materials are written by Indian authors and are specially oriented to Indian conditions and the needs of the Indian students.
(ii) Further development of the programmes of text-book production for the school stage under the NCERT.
(iii) Development of text-book production programme for the school stage under the State governments through the establishment of autonomous organizations and the development of research in curriculum and text-book production.

(D) Supply of Science Text-books

It is not enough to produce better text-books and supplementary reading materials but it is also necessary to ensure that these books become available to all students in time. This can be a major programme for quality improvement. For the improvement of the curriculum, we have to take the following points into consideration besides the text-books (Teacher Education, April-1969):

- We should create feeling of 'need' for improving the curriculum.
- We should determine a comprehensive organisational structure for curriculum improvement.

- We should determine the general design of the curriculum.
- We should discover and organize resource materials for instruction.
- We should develop working principle for dealing with child and adolescent development and learning.
- We should set-up a comprehensive and continuous evaluation programme.

1.4 HISTORICAL PERSPECTIVES OF SCIENCE EDUCATION IN INDIA

1.4.1 Development of Science Education after Independence

The Report of the Secondary Education Commission (1952-53) recommended the teaching of General Science as a compulsory subject in the High and Higher Secondary Schools. In the year 1956 the All India Seminar on Teaching of Science in Secondary Schools held at Tara Devi (Shimla Hills) dealt with almost all the problems facing the inclusion of General Science as a core subject for the Higher Secondary classes. It was the first of its kind which touched almost all aspects concerning the teaching of science in schools, viz. syllabus, equipment and apparatus, methods of examination, teaching aids in science and other allied matters like Text-books, Science Clubs, Museum, etc. It had suggested a unique and uniform system of science teaching for the entire country, suited to its needs and resources.

The Indian Parliamentary and Scientific Committee (IPSC) was set-up in August, 1961 under the chairmanship of Sri Lalbahadur Shastri to study the problems of "Science Education in Schools" with a view to find out the relation between the policies and decisions of the Centre and the States in the matter of science courses offered in the schools.

In 1963, The USSR Experts of the UNESCO Planning Mission visited India to study the implementation of technical assistance projects in the country. They worked on the problems from 3rd December, 1963 to 10th March, 1964 and gave their recommendations on different issues of science education in secondary schools. Three reports were prepared by the team which gave a total picture of the position of science and mathematics education in Indian and suggested ways to improve it. As a follow-up programme of the Report of UNESCO Planning Mission of Experts the Department of Science Education in the National Council took up some pilot projects for preparing new curriculum, text books, teacher's guides, etc. To start with, these experimental projects were started in about 20 selected schools in Delhi.

In the year 1964 the Education Commission was set-up under the chairmanship of Dr. D.S Kothari for up-grading school curricula with researches on curriculum developments, the revision of the text-books and teaching and learning materials. The Commission recommended that:

- Science and mathematics should be taught on a compulsory basis to all pupils as a part of general education during the first ten years of schooling.
- In the lower primary classes, science teaching should be related to the child's environment. The Roman alphabets should be taught in Class IV to facilitate understanding of internationally accepted symbols of scientific measurement and use of maps, charts and statistical tests.
- At the higher primary stage emphasis should be on the acquisition of knowledge and the ability to think logically, to draw conclusions and to make decisions at a higher level. A disciplined approach to the teaching of science was expected to be more effective than the general instructions on scientific matters.
- A science corner in lower primary schools and a laboratory-*cum*-lecture room in higher primary schools are minimum essential requirements.
- At the lower Secondary stage, science should be developed as a discipline of the mind. The newer concepts of physics, chemistry and biology and the experimental approach to the learning of science should be stressed.
- Science courses at an advanced level may be provided for talented students in selected lower secondary schools with necessary facilities of staff and laboratory.
- Science teaching should be linked to agriculture in rural areas and to technology in urban areas.
- The methods of teaching science should be modernized stressing the investigatory approach and the understanding

of the basic principles, guide materials should be made available to help teachers to adopt this approach laboratory work will need considerable improvement. There should be flexibility in the curriculum in order to cater to the special needs of the gifted.

- The development of science must derive its nourishment from our cultural and spiritual heritage and not bypass it.
- At the university level better conditions for research should be provided.

As a follow-up to the Kothari Commission Reports, the Ministry of Education and Social Welfare appointed an expert group in 1973 to develop curriculum for the 10 + 2 pattern. The group drafted an approach paper in 1975. A publication entitled "The curriculum for the ten year school: A framework" was published by the NCERT which also laid down guidelines for preparing syllabi, text books and the materials in a phased manner. Materials for Classes IX and X were prepared relating to a few subjects for the 1975-76 session. The Central Board of Secondary Education, New Delhi adopted the text-books prepared by NCERT for Classes IX and X, the first batch of candidates appeared in the public examination for Class X held in April, 1977.

The NCERT was established on September 1, 1961 as an autonomous organisation with its headquarters in New Delhi. At the headquarters, it had the National Institute of Education (NIE) which was concerned with research, instruction and evaluation. A Central Science Workshop was also established under the NCERT to produce proto-types of school equipment and to develop low-cost kits for the primary and the middle school stage.

Through the various departments of NIE and the Regional Colleges of Education (at present Regional Institute of Education), the NCERT discharge its functions relating to the improvement of school education at all levels and also of teacher training in India. It also functions as the academic wing of the Ministry of Human Resource Development of the Government of India. It maintains a close liaison with the education departments and the schools in the different States and Union territories of India.

Some States have now established State Councils of Educational Research and Training (SCERT) on the pattern of the NCERT. In these States, SCERT incorporates the functions of the State Institutes of Science Education.

State Institutes of Science and Education (SISEs) have been set-up in most of the states with a view to improving the quality of science education in the schools. The main functions of these institutes are to provide in-service training to science teachers in the new developments in the field of science education, conduct research studies in science education in their respective states, provide guidance service in science to schools to take-up innovative programmes in science education and participate in the National Science Programme.

The syllabi and the text-books prepared by the NCERT, specially for Classes IX and X evoked a lot of criticism from parents, teachers and students for allegedly having the following defects:

- The scheme of examination contained too many subjects for students.
- Illustrations are not clear and adequate.
- The experiment did not find a proper place in the teaching-learning process in the new pattern of education, thus maintaining the same system of bookish education.

As a result of the criticism of the new syllabus and text books, the Union Ministry of Education and Social Welfare appointed a Review Committee in June, 1977 under the chairmanship of Shri Ishwarbhai J. Patel, Vice-Chancellor, Gujarat University. The Committee submitted its report in November, 1977 under the title "Report of the Review Committee on the Curriculum for the Ten Year School." The following were the terms of reference of the Committee:

- To review the stage-wise and subject-wise objectives identified in the NCERT document "The Curriculum for the 10 year School."
- To scrutinise the NCERT syllabus and text books, in the light of the review as mentioned above.
- To scrutinise the scheme of studies, as given in the said document, and examine whether any suitable modifications in either the scheme of studies on the timetable or both should be made and to propose suitable staffing pattern.

According to the National Policy on Education, 1986, science education would be strengthened so as to develop in the child, well-defined abilities and values such as the spirit of inquiry, creativity, objectivity, the courage to question and an aesthetic sensibility:

- Science education programmes will be designed to enable the learner to acquire problem-solving and decision-making skills and to discover the relationship of science with health, agriculture, industry and other aspects of daily life. Every effort will be made to extend science education to the vast numbers who have remained outside the pale of formal education.

According to Programme of Action of the National Policy on Education, 1992 the aim of teaching science at this stage is primarily directed towards problem-solving the decision-making through the learning of key concepts which cut across all the disciplines of science. The content of science should be organised on the basis of two guidelines, namely, contemporary science and the learning ability of the pupil. It should reflect that science is a continuing human endeavour and it is international in character and method. Learning science will be oriented to ensure that the learners discover the relationship of science with health, agriculture, industry and other aspects of daily life.

1.4.2 Development of Science Education in Orissa

In the early years, Science Education was introduced at the Primary School stage. As back as in the year 1930, science was introduced by Director of Public Instruction (DPI) of Orissa in the shape of nature observation. The syllabus at this stage comprised topics like "observation of flowers in the plant and certain common animals of the locality". The Sun-rise and Sun-set", "the Earth and Sky", "Work, energy and power", etc. In those days science was not introduced at secondary stage as a core subject (Mohanty, 1987). The Secondary Education Commission, 1952-53 recommended the teaching of General Science as a compulsory subject in the High and Higher Secondary Schools' prior to it the Board of Secondary Education (BSE), Orissa in the year 1947 introduced General Science as a compulsory subject in High and Higher Secondary Schools'. In those days the subjects of elementary physics and chemistry were introduced in the Secondary Schools as optional subjects. The NCERT introduced Research Science Syllabus in the year 1961. This influenced the Board of Secondary Education, Orissa (BSE) to revise the Science syllabus. As per the recommendation of the Ishwarbhai Patel Committee in 1977, science has been introduced from Class II of the present 10 years schooling. The present science syllabus has undergone many major changes to accommodate recent inventions and discoveries in the field of modern science.

The State Council of Education Research and Training (SCERT) has undertaken experimental projects in the teaching of science at the Primary level under the title of "UNICEF-assisted Science Teaching Project" in Orissa.

The BSE Orissa appointed a group of experts to study the problems of different subjects including science subjects in the school curriculum. This expert group was appointed in the year 1953 to look into the proper teaching of science in schools.

There has been considerable expansion of science education at the University level also in addition to improvement of Science Education at the school stage. Utkal University was established in 1934 and subsequently in 1966 two more Universities—Sambalpur University and Berhampur University were established for general education. At present, Utkal University has teaching departments in science subjects of Physics, Chemistry, Botany, Zoology, Geology, Anthropology, Geography, Applied Psychology and mathematics.

The Orissa University of Agriculture & Technology (OUAT) situated at Bhubaneswar, has been providing under-graduate and post-graduate teaching in Agriculture, Veterinary, Fisheries, Forestry and allied subjects. Research wing of this university has done wonders in the field of modern Agriculture, Animal Husbandary, Fisheries and Forestry, etc. during the past several years.

In the field of secondary school science, some progress has been achieved since the introduction of general science at secondary level. Government of India sanctioned grants to High Schools for construction of science rooms and laboratories in phases. Grants for science equipments were also paid to the schools following a fixed standard. The establishment of the Regional College of Education (at present Regional Institute of Education) at Bhubaneswar in 1964 has also advanced the cause of Science Teacher Training Programme in Orissa. The summer programme has also been extended to the Primary school teachers and as such many science teachers are produced by this college for the elementary and secondary schools.

Orissa was benefited from the summer-courses in Physics, Chemistry and Biology organised by the NCERT and other agencies in the leading science colleges of Orissa. In such courses experts in teaching in science from the United States were involved on behalf of the UNESCO.

During the 1960's science club movement spread in Orissa in a big way and many High Schools started their science clubs. State level Science Fairs have been a yearly programme since then in which high school and primary school students participate with their exhibits under the guidance of their science teachers.

Many Research Institutes in Science have been set-up in Orissa. The Central Rice Research Institute (CRRI) of Cuttack is one of the making inventions and innovations pioneering institution. The Regional Research Laboratory (RRL) at Bhubaneswar is one of few such organisations in the country. It provides scope for carrying on research activities by a number of scientists of the state. The Physics Institute, Life Science Institute and Central Institute of Freshwater Acquaculture (CIFA) of Bhubaneswar are high level bodies for research works in the area of Physics, Life Science, Fisheries and Fresh Water Pearl Culture.

In the present school curriculum, science is taught as General Science. In the State Council of Educational Research and Training various steps are being taken to popularise science education at the school stage. As per the plan of operation the state government appointed science supervisors in each district to take care of implementation of the science curriculum at the primary, middle and secondary level.

Under the State Education Department, the Science Museum at Bhubaneswar possesses mobile science vans. Which are equipped with science experiments and apparatus. These are utilized in science exhibitions for demonstration of experiments organised at centrally placed schools through the SCERT, Orissa. There are several benefits from the mobile science vans. Mobile Science Vans move round the State and demonstrate the complicated principles of school science in different schools of the State on proper invitations.

The Birla Institute of Technical Museum (BITM), Calcutta is also doing a pioneering work in the field of school science education by conducting Eastern India Science Camp in its campus for school children. It provides also mobile science vans to different schools at different times in the State of Orissa, to popularise science teaching and learning so as to develop scientific temper and attitude in young learners.

The SCERT every year organises state level science exhibition and other activities relating to science teaching and learning to popularise science among young learners. The Inspector of Schools by the help of the science supervisors organise district level science exhibitions and other activities so as to encourage the teachers and students (elementary and secondary levels) participation. The Inspectors of Schools select the best exhibits from their respective districts and send them to state-level science fair is organised by SCERT. The SCERT holds every year an Annual Science Fair at different places of the state and invites the district level talents to exhibit their work. Through the fair the better talents are selected and are sent to national and regional level science fair conducted by the NCERT and the BITM respectively.

Besides this the Department of Forest and Environment, Government of Orissa, the Regional Science Centre, Bhubaneswar and the Planetorium Bhubaneswar organise regularly different activities related to environment protection, problem of pollution and other science teaching-learning activities to create awareness among school students. The talents are being honoured and this also helps a young learner to be aware of maintaining equilibrium in the ecosystem.

The Institutes of Advanced Studies in Education and Colleges of Teacher Education are also actively engaged with the pre-service science teacher training programmes so as to produce quality science teachers for secondary level. The teacher training curriculum in the state is under constant process of revision so as to accommodate recent developments in the field of science teaching and learning. The District Institutes of Education and Training (DIET) are actively involved in the upliftment of science education at the elementary level. The pre-service as well as in-service teacher training programmes are being conducted by DIETs regularly to improve the quality of science education in the State.

The Orissa Vijnan Academy, Bhubaneswar also publishes magazines and organises other activities to popularise science and bring about awareness about the environment among masses and the young learners.

In the light of NPE-1986 the school curriculum was revised in our state. This revision was made as per new directions given by NPE-1986 for the reorientation of the content and process of education. In order to initiate curricular efforts for promotion of national pattern of education, the national curriculum framework for primary and secondary level developed by NCERT identified ten common core components, which are sought to be made obligatory for all schools in the country. One such core component is inculcation of the scientific temper. In order to actualize the provisions of NPE-1986 the science-education was given more emphasis in school curriculum.

The Board of Secondary Education (BSE), Orissa, introduced two science text-books for each of Classes-IX and X, Part-I that is "Madhyamika Vijnan, Pratham Bhag" deals with physical science and Part-II deals with biological sciences. In Class-IX, the new science text-books were introduced in the academic year 1988-89. Since the introduction of the new books many objections have been raised by teachers as to the effectiveness of the text-books within the scheduled time frame. The BSE has been organising intermittently orientation programmes in science, workshop on science teaching, refresher courses in science and science teaching to overcome the problems of science teaching in secondary schools.

Regional Institute of Education (RIE), Bhubaneswar has been undertaking many extension programmes for in-service secondary as well as elementary school teachers since its inception. Through those programmes a sizeable number of teachers were equipped with knowledge of recent development in the various branches of science as well as in the field of science teaching.

1.5 EMERGENCE AND NEED

In this age of scientific and technological advancement everybody should have atleast some basic knowledge of science for making effective and useful contribution to life. A citizen of modern world sees manifestations of science all around him. There is no sphere of man's life today which has not been influenced by science in one way or the other. This is because we are living in an age of "scientific culture." Science has shrunk the world and it has totally changed the human outlook. Modern science is no longer confined to the surface of this globe.

A critical appraisal of Science Education Programme at the secondary level is highly essential because of its ever changing nature to evaluate the relevance of curriculum to assess the status of laboratory facilities and teaching methodology and over all performance of science teacher in secondary schools.

Science is not just a collection of some isolated and assorted facts and principles. Moreover, knowledge is not static. It may change its meaning and importance with time. Science is to be made meaningful and valuable, should be taught as a whole at the school stage. The objective of Science should be reflected in the curriculum of secondary schools. Science has opened innumerable avenues for pursuing different vocations. A student of science can study engineering and technology, medicine, agriculture, veterinary science and animal husbandary or any similar subject and make his career in that profession.

The study explores different facets of problems related to science teaching in secondary schools of Orissa. Science is the key to all development. It has brought a revolutionary change in the world and the social life of individuals. A positive attitude should be developed among the students towards science and technology from secondary school level which is really not found with the present day learners. The curriculum of secondary school is not able to reveal appropriately the importance of science in education.

Science teaching needs both infrastructural and methodological upgradation of curricular improvement as a major area to be highlighted to ensure good science education. The mushroom growth of secondary schools especially by private bodies in recent years has rendered the science education helpless and neglected. Due to lack of fund for laboratory expenses chemicals, etc. job insecurity of science teacher and laboratory assistants have further aggravated the situation. Even in most of the Government Schools the negligence of authority and indifferent attitude of teachers have made the situation worse.

This study intends to unfold several complexities involved in science teaching from different angles, i.e. curriculum, method of teaching, teachers training and laboratory facilities, etc. This study is highly essential to ensure the standard and status of science education in the state of Orissa. A developing country like India needs rapid improvement of science education to inculcate scientific spirit among the students. The present study would reveal the status of science education secondary in schools of Orissa affiliated to the Board of Secondary Education (BSE), Cuttack, Orissa and the Central Board of Secondary Education (CBSE), New Delhi. The insight into the varied problems of science teaching, curriculum and laboratory, etc. has to be developed through the study. A critical appraisal can be done only when the existing resources are thoroughly assessed with a view to harnessing them for future development.

Teaching is a complex process in which laboratory, teaching aids and teacher get involved with equal importance. The standard of science teaching should be updated with the changing needs of society and diffusion of knowledge. In a class room teaching-learning situation there is a constant interaction between the teacher and the taught. Teacher's classroom activities are therefore, performed in a socio-cultural setting, that is in a social environment. Science teacher gives new scientific idea and knowledge to students in the school situation. Secondary school teachers have special importance as secondary education is an important stage of students' career. There are several problems faced by the science teacher in classroom situation. These problems are not solved yet. This study is supposed to reveal in detail the deficiencies and difficulties in Science Education in the secondary schools of Orissa.

1.6 STATEMENT OF THE PROBLEM

In an economically backward State like Orissa, an investigation into the present position of science teaching programme has got special importance. The study is intended to spot out the defects and assess the relevance of the present science education programme at the secondary level.

Hence, the problem decided to be investigated is "A Critical Appraisal of Science Education Programme at Secondary level."

1.7 OBJECTIVES

The objectives of the study are as detailed:

(i) To make a survey of the existing provisions and facilities available for organising Science Education programme in secondary schools of Orissa.

(ii) To find out the lacunae and deficiencies in the Science Education programme which is in vogue to meet the requirement of secondary school students.

(iii) To identify the strengths and good practices in the system.

(iv) To pool the views and suggestions of the teachers, supervisors and educationists in order to suggest remedies for removed of the deficiencies.

(v) To recommend the measures for improving the Science Education programme in secondary schools.

2

Studies in Science Education in Schools

2.1 INTRODUCTION

Study of related literature implies locating, reading and evaluating reports of research. It is also causal observation and opinion that are related to individuals' planned research project. A documentary study may require data gleaned from a great variety of published sources. The scholar must be familiar both with the standard reference guides in his own field and with general guides and listings.

Importance of Review of Related Literature

In order to make the study worthwhile, it is required to make a comprehensive survey of the studies that have already been done pertaining to the problem and its related aspects. Aggarwal (1975) has listed eleven important reasons for which review of related studies should be made:

- The review of literature is the basis of most of the research projects in the Physical Sciences, Natural Sciences, Social Sciences and Humanities.
- A review of the related literature gives the scholar an understanding of the precious work that has been done.
- The result of the review actually provides the data used in the research.
- It enables us to know the means of getting to the frontier in the field of our problems, while we have learn what others have done and what still remains to be done in our area. We cannot develop a research project that will contribute to furthering.

- A review of the literature would be develop the insight of the investigator, the information thus gained will save the researcher's much time.
- The importance of the review is quite obvious in delimiting the research problem and of defining it better.
- The review of the literature will give the student the insight he needs to convert his tentative research problems to a specific and concise one.
- A review of the literature can help the research worker in making him alert to research possibilities that have been overlooked.
- In the process of reviewing the literature the student is on the alert for finding out research approaches in his area that have proved to be sterile.
- The review of the literature provides with an opportunity of gaining insight into the methods to measures, subjects and approaches employed by other research workers. This in turn will lead to significant improvement of research design.
- A careful consideration of the chapter entitled 'Recommendation for further Research' in various research studies, guides the investigator regarding the suitability of a problem and delimiting the research problems.

As a matter of fact, the significance of related literature cannot be denied in any research work because without it, the research study can not claim to be full fledged one. Realising the importance Good, Barr and Scates (1941) have stated that: " The competent physician must keep abreast of the latest discoveries in the field of medicine. Obviously the careful student of education, the research worker and investigator should become familiar with the location and use of sources of educational information."

For any worthwhile study, a review of related literature is of immense help to the researcher. The studies related to this problem have been reviewed under three categories, such as International, National and State levels.

2.2 STUDIES AT INTERNATIONAL LEVEL

Research in foreign countries varies from sophisticated studies of limited scope that employ modern statistical techniques to broad assessments, status studies and evaluation of course improvement project. Much of the research reported in journals generally available in this county is essentially of three types:

(1) Comparative studies between the United States and one or more other countries,
(2) Studies of the status of Science Education in foreign countries, and
(3) General assessment of science education with proposals for modification that are usually based on an examination of national goals, indigenous values and similar sociological, psychological and philosophical bases.

These have been done most commonly by nationals working in doctoral dissertations in United States Universities. Sangulang's study (1961) was based on the explicit assumption that rural science education in the Philippines should directly minister to do the more urgent needs of rural life. Health and increase in farm production were, for example, the most urgent needs on his list. Herandez (1960) had also done work in order to determine the direction that science education should contribute to the solution of social problems including the raising of the standard of living. The study was essentially philosophical and intuitive and resulted in conclusions that derived inevitably from the main assumption.

Khalid (1954) stated a proposal for the reconstruction of Iraqi Science Education which would foster the improvement of individual and societal conditions. His procedures included an analysis of Iraqi society including consideration of the major social problems towards the solving of which science education might presumably make a contribution. This was followed by an analysis of science education in Iraq and a proposed scheme for the reconstruction of science education in terms of objectives, content, teaching method, examinations and the preparation of science teachers, educationists and other professionals to up grade and improve the Science Education (as reported in Science Education Newsletter No. 45, May, 1981). As a result of which attempts were underway to establish a Spanish Association for Science Education. The main objectives of the Association were:

- To facilitate the exchange of opinion on Science Education.

- To notify, co-ordinate and facilitate the implementation of work carried out in the field of Science Education.
- To notify seminars, courses, meetings and journals in the science education field in Spain and abroad.

In Britain the University of Oxford, Department of Educational Studies offers to well qualified and experienced teachers and lecturers a one-year full time course for the degree of Master of Science Education (Science Education Newsletters No. 43, Sept. 1980). All science education students take courses titled; Curriculum Studies in Science, and Measurement and Experimental Design, under the general heading of science education. The general heading of Science Education provisions are made for teachers of the experimental sciences, mathematics and geography using a system of general seminars with specialist follow-up in subject areas.

The aims of the Science Education Support Centres in Srilanka (Science Education Newsletter No. 45, May 1981) are:

- To improve the science background of teachers according to their individual need.
- To encourage teachers to adapt realistic methods of teaching science and actively involving their pupils in experiment and investigation.
- To encourage teachers to use the environment of the school.
- To enrich their science teaching at the centres in ways considered by the staff to be a good teaching practice.

In 1949, Bullington's study reveals a general science course, most commonly offered programme in the colleges and universities in United States. That programme consisted of two separate courses, i.e. Biological Science and Physical Science. In 1952, Bullington's another study revealed that increasing number of institutions were offerings survey mode of research programmes in the field of science education.

Subsequently it was found from Badgley's (1956) questionnaire that most respondent considered that integration was provided by attention to interrelations within a given subject matter and among other fields.

Hall and others (1961) emphasised that cognitive process be given special importance at the elementary school level. Thereafter a great deal of studies conducted on behavioural aspects of science students and variation of content in science curriculum. Quantitative experimental work is emphasised in the laboratory and taxonomic word and drawing has been deemphasised on a study conducted by Moore (1965).

Gagne (1966) emphasised that the major efforts should be given to the identifications of "PROCESS SKILLS" and their inclusion in school programmes. Subsequently importance was given on gradual improvement of science curricula through projects and research works.

According to Rowe (1969) the teacher's role is guiding the thinking of his students is critically important. The teachers with sensitivity and thorough understanding of their subject matter are highly effective in teaching science.

The status of science education and its trend emphasised on change in science teaching in school after 1970 in Bangladesh. The studies conducted in early eighties were both evaluative and developmental in nature. The curricular framework in teacher training evaluative and developmental in nature. The curricular framework in teacher training evaluation emphasised for the improvement of school curriculum.

At the International level, the implications of science teaching in schools have already been viewed from different angles to bring the desirable change in the curriculum method of teaching, evaluation and teacher training respectively. Few studies at international level are worth mentioning here.

The studies of the status of general education in science courses were conducted by Bullington (1949). The major findings of this investigation were that more than half of the four year colleges and universities in the United States offered some kind of general education in science courses. The most commonly offered programme consisted of two separate courses, one was the biological science and another was physical sciences. A survey of subject matter was the most common approach with a block and gap approach a study of selected problems and historical approach respectively the next most popular methods organising the courses Bullington (1952) conducted another study few years latter and found that an increasing number of institutions were offering survey type research programmes in the area of science education.

Badgley (1956) developed a questionnaire to determine the nature of general studies curricula in science and mathematics throughout the United States. His sample consist of 140 institutions and 80 per cent of them were responded it. He found that many institutes had adopted a two year general education course but the great majority required basic introductory courses in specific science fields. Most respondents considered that integration was provided by attention to interrelations within a given subject matter and among other fields. This was commonly accomplished by means of a prescribed core of liberal arts courses with 12 semester hours of such work being a common requirement of general education purposes. Although a few integrated courses were used, these were restricted to small basic course in general studies programmes.

The American Association for the Advancement of Science (Hall *et al*. 1961) sponsored a major study designed to review the status of elementary school science and formulate a plan for improvements. This report stressed that "Cognitive Processes" be given special emphasis at the elementary school level.

Davis (1962) studied the introductory Biology programmes in Junior Colleges of Texas in the Biological Science, which was developed under the auspices of the National Academy of Science and the National Research Council. He found that these introductory programmes were typically a Botany-Zoology combination, that the teaching methods consisted largely of specific descriptions that the laboratory work involved mainly dissection and drawing of preserved specimens and there was a vast discrepancy between the programme found in Texas Junior College and the programme recommended by the National Research Council.

Watoson (1963) has reported a comprehensive survey of research on classification instruction in science. He was particularly interested in investigations of possible relationship between the behaviour of science students over and extensive range of outcomes, pointing out that the broad objectives for science teaching are seldom explicated in research conducted in a class room context.

Moore (1965) conducted a study and the major findings of the study were the following:

(1) There was a great variation of contents, with two-thirds of the respondents reporting recent changes with less phylogeny and more physiology and cellular and molecular biology.

(2) Introductory Biology courses throughout the nation were in a state of flux.
(3) Out of the 32 colleges sampled, 15 were giving a single introductory course, 8 were giving two courses, 6 were giving three courses, 3 were giving four courses and 28 of the colleges were providing at least, one course that is combined Botany and Zoology.
(4) The courses were organised around subjects such as molecular biology and physiology and use such general themes as evolution and ecology.
(5) Quantitative experimental work was emphasized in the laboratory and taxonomic work and drawing has been deemphasized.

Woodburn and Obourn (1965) described science education in American Schools during the eighteenth and nineteenth centuries by identifying the major distinctive periods and highlighting significant reports. The development of high school science on a broad scale dated from 1872, when Harvard college began accepting science courses for college entrance.

According to Rowe (1969) the teacher's role in guiding the thinking of his students critically was important in the learning process, especially when he was dealing with so-called slow learners. It has been demonstrated on numerous occasions that teachers with sensitivity and a thorough understanding of their subject matter were highly effective in teaching science to these students. When guided by such teachers, most of the student no longer exhibited the behaviours which caused them to be classified as slow learners in the first place.

The applications of science to society are as important as the content of science and the processes of science. The nature of science is related to the social, moral, ethical consequences of science.

In 1976, the National Science Foundation (NSF) found three major research efforts to ascertain the current status of science education and to describe trends or patterns that existed in these practices. One of these three studies was a literature review of the relevant research in science education by Helgeson, Blosser and Howe (1977). Second was a national survey of current practices by Weiss (1978) and third was a series of in-depth case study in which researchers spent an extended amount of time in the public schools and their communities to identify current practices by Stake and Easley (1978). From the baseline data provided by these three approaches it was anticipated that policy could be generated regarding future federal priorities in supporting Science Education. Significant patterns emerged from these studies regarding schooling practices and procedures, the education of science teachers and the influence of political control of education.

Muttaque (1981) conducted a study on development of curriculum in Biology for secondary schools of Bangladesh:

(i) The major findings of the study were in the formative evaluation the curricular and co-curricular materials were found suitable and appropriate for the purpose of the study.

(ii) The curricular materials were effective line producing significant gain in knowledge of the students about ecological facts, principles, information and related problems as well as their possible solutions.

(iii) The curricular materials were effective in producing significant changes in attitudes towards environment in the majority of the grades.

(iv) The teacher's manual was effective in producing significant positive changes in the attitudes of teachers.

(v) The teacher's manual was effective in producing significant ecological facts and related problems with possible solutions.

(vi) There was low correlation between the gain in ecological knowledge and the change in attitude towards environment.

(vii) Rural students possessed significantly less ecological knowledge.

(viii) In two grades the rural students showed more favourable attitudes towards environment than the urban students of the same grades while in the majority of grades there was no significant difference in the mean gain in achievement of the rural and the urban students with respect to mean gain in attitudes.

(ix) There was significant difference in the level of ecological knowledge of boys and girls. The girls possessed more knowledge than the boys.

(x) In the majority of the grades there were no difference in attitudes of boys and girls towards environments.

(xi) In the majority of the grades the difference between the rural and the urban boys in respect of knowledge in ecology was significant. The knowledge in ecology of urban boys was better.

(xii) The difference between the rural and the urban boys in respect of attitudes towards ecology was significant.

(xiii) Significant difference between the rural and urban girls in respect of ecological difference knowledge, the urban girls possessed more ecological knowledge.

(xiv) The difference in attitudes towards environment between the rural and the urban girls was significant. In the majority of the grades the urban girls possessed more favourable attitudes in the majority of the grade.

2.3 STUDIES AT NATIONAL LEVEL

Trends of Research in Science Education at National Level

The frequency of researches in the field of science education in India by the end of Fifth Survey of Educational Research (1988-92) was just meagre. The researches in various areas of science education along unilateral classification have been presented in Tables 2.1 and 2.2.

TABLE 2.1

Frequency of Researches Conducted in Various Areas of Science Education

Sl No.	*Area of Science Education*	*No. of Studies*
1.	Philosophy of Science/Scientific method/Nature of Science	—
2.	Historical Studies including Comparative studies in Science Education	—
3.	Policy Studies	—
4.	Environmental Studies	9
5.	Science Curriculum Syllabus and Text-book	7
6.	Learning Science and Models of Teaching	15
7.	Teaching Strategies	4
8.	Outcomes of Science Education Scientific Temper, attitudes, skills and interests	8
9.	Correlates of Achievement in Science	7
10.	Educational Technology	3
11.	Other Studies of interest	8
	Total	**61**

Source: Fifth Survey of Educational Research, 1988-92, Vol. I, 1997, NCERT.

TABLE 2.2

Frequency of Researches Conducted at Various Levels

Sl. No.	*Level of Research*	*No. of Studies*
1.	Master of Philosophy	05
2.	Doctor of Philosophy	34
3.	Research Papers	06
4.	Independent projects/Studies	16
	Total	**61**

Source: Fifth Survey of Educational Research, 1988-92, Vol. I, 1997, NCERT.

In the field of science education the contribution made by the NCERT, New Delhi, her counterparts in the States of the Union, i.e. SCERT and All India Science Teachers' Association, New Delhi, as well as some voluntary organisation such as the Hoshungabad Science Teaching Project in Madhya Pradesh etc. are significant. Lastly taking an overall view, the benefit provided by published researches, methods, texts, teachers guides, production of scientific equipment and educational journal magazines such as School Science, Junior Science Digest, Science Reporter and many other in different regional languages of our country are also immense.

The review of researches by Vaidya (1997) in Fifth Survey of Educational Research (1988-92) in Science Education in the area of environmental studies the researchers visualise two sets of studies. Firstly, the environment is explored in its content; and secondly, it is explored as a teaching-learning resource in a wider setting. Regardless of the method of exploration or purpose, both the modes can be bent faithfully for educational purposes right from primary education through secondary education to even higher education, including teacher education.

In the area of science curriculum, syllabus and text-books it was in 1950 that Kelkar for the first time developed a curriculum in general science for secondary schools. Veerappa (1958) for the first time sought to compare the position of science education in India and assessed the developing trends on the basis of observations made by researches in USA and UK. He studied the feasibility of introducing the trends followed in USA and UK in India institution in teaching science through Herbartian Plane. Lecture, Lecture-*cum*-Demonstration Method and Essay Type questions in examinations were then trends.

Patole (1967) undertook a study to explore the existing weakness of teaching in rural areas and advised methods for improving it. Activity method was found superior to traditional method.

Sheth (1967) studied the achievement of the secondary school students and found boys were achieving more than girls. The NCERT conducted nine studies during 1970-72 as regards to text-books and evaluation procedure in subjects like Mother Tongue, Physics, English, History, Geography, General Science, Social Studies, Chemistry and Biology to develop the basic principles and procedures in the preparation and evaluation of text-books in the above mentioned subjects.

Jha (1970) examined the nature of relationship between the intelligence and aptitude of children. Nayar (1971) studied on the achievement of the students on the science.

Singh (1977) studied the standard of science curriculum A systematic comparison between old and new science curriculum was studied by SCERT Andhra Pradesh (1980). Ramdas (1981) emphasised on formulation of objectives of science teaching in classroom.

Bandyopadhyay (1984) assessed the students attitude towards science. He also examined the environmental and academic factors that influence the attitude of students towards science. Barman (1983) studied the origin and development of modern science in pre-Independent India. Sharma (1984) evaluated the science education in secondary schools its status and access of general people to it before Independence. He reviewed systematically the history of science curricular in different times after Independence.

Later on as reported in Fifth Survey of Educational Research (1988-92) other studies appeared with different approaches in mind. These approaches were by Vaidya, N (Concept-based plus children inquires about the environment, 1989), Ganguli and Vashistha (1991) and Ramesh (objective-based curriculum, 1984) and finally Vashistha (Biology within the context of mechanistic and organism viewpoints, 1986).

Then during eighties and early nineties appeared several studies of varying interest in the area of curriculum and evaluation by Ganguli and Vashistha (1991), Krishnan (1981), Goyal (1982), Arora (1986) and Khalwania (1986). Menon (1986) examined the science education system of Gujarat State from the view point of science as inquiry.

Some researchers tried to study in the area of learning and models of teaching in science. Awasthi (1989) developed a fruitful training strategy for science teaching, using the concept attainment model, Aziz (1990) examined the effectiveness of information processing models on acquiring chemical concepts, Kayathri (1989) showed the effectiveness of the Jerry Luces Memory Model in Botany and that too in a real school setting.

Few researches focused light on usefulness of the different teaching strategies in science in real class room setting. Aranha (1988) showed the utility of Mastery Learning approach for slow learners. They gained in scores on final tests along with strong academic motivation and self-concept habits. Gurumurthy (1990) found the guided discovery approach superior to the instructed performance and when it came to the development of cognitive abilities and practical skills. Goel and Agbebi (1990) reported that the acquisition of Psychomotor skills favoured the group which followed the individual laboratory method rather than Lecture-*cum*-Demonstration Method.

Scientific temper, attitudes, skills and interests are the outcome of effective science education. Few researches have also been conducted in this field which show that all groups of students showed scientific temper (Dubey, 1992) all students from urban and rural areas possess favourable attitude towards the science curriculum and effective academic programmes develop favourable attitudes towards science curriculum (Mandlia, 1988). Scientific aptitude is related scientific attitude (Ghose, 1989) development of scientific attitudes depend upon their perception of science teaching and nature of learning experiences (Kumar, 1991) various components of the learning environment are significantly related to both scientific attitudes and interests, there is significant relationship between the public understanding of science and attitude towards science (Sood, 1992).

Kelkar (1950) conducted a study entitled "Tentative Course of Study in General Science" which reveals the following:

(i) High School pupils were more interested in science than in any other subject.
(ii) The boys were more interested in science than girls.
(iii) Pupils' interest in science no more in the beginning but it decreased as the course advanced.
(iv) The interest was evenly divided between Biological and Physical Sciences.

(v) There was no significant difference in the distribution of pupils' scientific interest between the Biological and Physical Sciences.

(vi) The scientific interest of pupils of both the sexes were at the high school stage were more in topics based on health and physiological, plant life and astronomy.

(vii) Soil bacteria, air and water were topic in which high school pupils showed the list interest.

(viii) High School pupils were found to be more interested in the fundamental of the science than in its practical application.

The suggested course in general science consisted of ten units each of which represented some major problems of living covering a wide area of human experience and some important aspect of his environment.

Veerappa (1958) conducted a study to examine the position of science education in India and assessed the developing trends on the basis of observations in the U.S.A., UK, etc. The feasibility of introducing the trends in Indian institutions was also investigated. He found that teaching science through Herbrtian Plans, the Lecture-*cum*-Demonstration Method and essay type evaluation in the examination were the trends at that time.

Buch, *et al.* (1960) in Gujarat and Rup Prakash (1968) in Punjab and Haryana developed achievement tests in general science for grade VIII. In these studies the usual methods of finding reliability co-efficient were used and the co-efficients were in general around 0.90. They found correlation between the achievement in science and location of the schools where the students study. The findings indicated significant difference in the achievements of pupils in science. Pupils in urban areas scored more than the pupils in rural areas.

Patole (1967) undertook and study to explore the existing weakness of teaching science in primary schools and devised methods for improvement in the existing situation. It was limited to rural areas mainly and the following were some of the important findings:

(i) About seventy-four per cent teachers and sixty-one per cent trainees were of the opinion that science should be a separate subject from standard (I) and should not be integrated with social studies in the first four grades.

(ii) Sixty per cent of the teachers had passed their primary school certificate examination, thirty-nine per cent had passed the secondary school certificate examination and the remaining have taken higher education.

(iii) The average number of pupils per teacher in standard (I) was 73.40 which gradually decreased in higher standards and in standard VII it came upto 27.27.

(iv) Only ten schools possessed complete set of the equipment for the practical demonstration of experiments.

(v) None of the schools had a separate science room.

(vi) None of the schools subscribed to any periodical devoted to scientific knowledge and information.

(vii) There was no significant difference between the boys and girls as regards interest in science.

(viii) The number of questions asked by pupils decreased as they advanced in age.

(ix) The topic in which pupils showed interest were our body, health and hygiene, machines, diseases, heat senses, air, water, food and plants.

(x) The topic in which pupils showed less interest were pests on plants seasons insects, fishes and other animals, reproduction of human beings.

(xi) The activity-based method was found superior to the traditional one.

It was revealed from the study conducted by Sheth (1967) that:

(i) The reliability co-efficients of the achievement tests as calculated by the three methods varied from 0.888 to 0.985 for grade (V) from 0.894 to 0.991 for grade (VI) and from 0.932 to 0.985 for grade (VII).

(ii) The validity co-efficients of the tests against teachers' ratings varied from 0.56 to 0.89.

(iii) The validity co-efficient of the tests against school annual examination marks in general science ranged from 0.516 to 0.832.

(iv) The predictive validity co-efficients for the annual examination marks obtained from the same sample ranged from 0.56 to 0.89.

(v) Boys were significantly higher in achievement than girls.

The important findings of the study conducted by Gisler (1967) is upgrading and continuous progress in teacher education materials, facilities, methodology and curriculum planning are some of basic keys to successful and fruitful science education for all students.

The study of Jha (1970) examined the nature of relationship between intelligence, scientific aptitude, adjustment, anxiety, extroversion, study habits and socio-economic status on one hand and achievement in science on the other. Following were some of the findings:

(i) There was significant positive relationship between achievement in science and (a) general intelligence, (b) scientific aptitude, and (c) adjustment.
(ii) There was significant negative relationship between achievements in science and anxiety in the case of boys and combined samples but not so in the case of girls.
(iii) There was no relationship between achievement in science and extroversion.
(iv) There was significant positive relationship between achievements in science and study habits in the case of boys and combined samples, but not so in the case of girls.
(v) There was no relationship between achievement in science and socio-economic status.

The study by Nayar (1971) attempted to predict achievement in science with the help of following six variables such as in verbal reasoning ability, numerical ability, comprehension and interpretation, problem-solving, critical thinking ability and spatial ability. Factor analysis at the correlation matrix of the above variable was also carried out to study the amount of variance that could be attributed to aptitude for science. The main findings were:

(i) The difference between the mean scores of boys and girls on numerical ability, problem-solving and critical thinking, appraisal tests were significant at 0.1 level, boys being superior.
(ii) There was however no significant difference between the mean performance of rural and urban students on the six experimental and the criterion variables.

(iii) The cor-relation co-efficient between the scores on critical thinking criterion, in case at boys was significant at 0.05 level.

(iv) There were significant differences at 0.05 level between boys and girls in their cor-relations in Verbal Reasoning Test of the NCERT, and comprehension and Interpretation of the Educational Testing Service Cooperative Science Test, girls being superior in both the cases.

(v) The multiple co-relation co-efficients were, Numerical Ability Test and Verbal Reasoning Test, 0.6005, Numerical Ability, Verbal Reasoning and Cooperative Science, 0.6383 and Numerical Ability, Verbal Reasoning, Cooperative Science and the revised Minnesota Paper Board Test (FB) 0.6525.

(vi) The variances of the four tests for school science were 15.6 per cent Numerical Ability, 13.6 per cent Verbal Reasoning, 19.5 per cent Cooperative Science and 5.6 per cent Minnesota Paper Board Test.

(vii) These four tests had highest validity of any combination at tests chosen from the six tests used.

(viii) Three common factors were revealed in this study, which have been named as General factor 'g' Conceptual Facility and Numerical Facility.

(ix) The study revealed agreement, to a great extent, between the findings obtained through multiple cor-relation and through factor analysis.

The major findings of the study conducted by Singh (1977) were:

(i) Significant difference between the means of achievement in knowledge objective was found on three out of six schools.

(ii) Significant difference between the means at achievement in skill objective was found in all the schools.

(iii) Significant difference between the means of achievements in application objective was found in five out of the six schools.

The investigator concluded that the curriculum suggested was more suitable than the existing science curriculum in force in the state needed modification.

The main findings of the study taken up by Sonar (1975) were as follows:

(i) Very few filmstrips produced and available at present in the country co-relate with syllabus and text book.
(ii) Filmstrips co-related with text and is regional languages and help to increase the knowledge of students.
(iii) Almost all topics in general science syllabus and the text-books can be effectively taught with the help of filmstrips.
(iv) The cost of filmstrips can be largely reduced if they are produced in large quantities.
(v) Systematic planning was essential in using filmstrips and filmstrip projectors in primary school teaching.
(vi) The use of these instructional aids indicated the possibility of improvement in the methodology of science teaching, raising the standard of science education in primary schools and development of test and interest in the younger generation for the science subjects.

The findings of the study conducted by SCERT. Andhra Pradesh (1980): On "Evaluation Study of Text Books in Environmental Studies of Classes III and V on Revised Curriculum in Science" were:

(i) Most of the headmasters and teachers felt that the old curriculum was not relevant to the child cognitive level as well as needs but contrary to this, parents felt that the old curriculum was easily understandable to the children.
(ii) The teachers and headmasters felt that the new curriculum was relevant to the environment in which the children lived, but the parents of the children felt that the new curriculum increased the cognitive load of the children.
(iii) According to the teachers and headmasters the new science curriculum fulfilled the educational objectives as prescribed by the Directorate of Education.
(iv) The headmasters felt that the new curriculum was relevant to the age level of the children. But the teachers and parents felt that the new curriculum was above the cognitive level of children of Classes III and V.
(v) The headmasters and the teachers opined that the new science curriculum was helpful in developing modernity

among pupils. The view of the parents did not indicate anything in this direction.

(vi) The teachers, parents and headmasters opined the new curriculum was more helpful than old one in enriching the knowledge of the children.

(vii) The parents, teachers and headmasters indicated that the new curriculum was relevant to the needs of the children.

The study conducted by Ramdas (1981) lead to some broad generalization. The comparison of the control and experimental groups revealed as follows:

(i) Teachers showed some significant changes such as willingness to change their teaching methods and want beyond the textual materials to include real life experiences and to encourage participation of pupils.

(ii) An improvement in the pupils ability to apply concepts in physics to non-textual situations was also observed.

(iii) There was no difference in the use of novel ideas of the experimental and the control groups. Pupils in the experimental group contributed more to discussions in the classroom, however, improvement of pupil in the skill of experimentation and their group activities was not significantly differ to in the two groups compared.

(iv) Suggestions were made to pay more attention to the actual process of education in the actual class room and bring about a conceptual change in its role, to study in the field actual effectiveness of the curricula and to adopt teaching method and curricula to the changing needs of the society.

The major findings as revealed by Krishnan (1981) were:

(i) The science curricula of the States of Kerala and Tamilnadu were both moderately satisfactory with respect to all dimensions except methodological instructional.

(ii) The science curricula of the two States did not satisfy most of the criteria prescribed for both traditional and modern science curricula.

(iii) The science curricula of both the Kerala state was better than that of Tamilnadu in meeting four criteria and fourteen sub-criteria developed for the study. While the latter was found superior in meeting two criteria and three sub-criteria.

(iv) The curricula of both the States were found weak in the dimensions of 'methodological-Instructional', understanding of the evolution of major concepts and systems of science and the instruction. The curriculum of Kerala was found to be additionally weak in provision of experiences for developing general manipulative skills and provision of teachers' hand books. The curriculum of Tamilnadu was found to be additionally weak in the provision of understanding of basic science-based social functions, provision for accepted forms of curricular organization representation to important scientific movements, basic laboratory work and comprehensive evaluation of learning outcome and provision of text-books and audio-visual materials.

(v) The two curricula did not give adequate importance to self-study or practical work. They were found to be too rigid to provide for meaningful experiences outside the classroom.

Barman (1983) studied the origin and development of modern science in pre-independent India. The major findings of the study taken up by Bandyopadhyay (1984) were:

(i) Pupils having high positive attitude towards science and a negative attitude towards science were different with respect to the independent variables either in isolation or in interaction.

(ii) The obtained casual factors were environmental, attitudinal and achievement-related. Parent education and socio-economic status led to favourable attitude towards science. Teacher's influence, peers' influence, vocational value of science and future aim of life were other contributory factory. The pupils who had a favourable attitude to science possessed higher ability in mechanical comprehension and visualisation of objects in space. They were higher achievers in physical and life science.

(iii) There existed significant interactions between (a) Source of inspiration and achievement in physical science, (b) Source, achievement in physical science and space reactions, and (c) Source achievements in life science and space relations.

Sharma (1984) conducted a study assuming that such a study of school science education policy over a period of 30 years of post-Independence would be of some value to the policy-makers and planners. It focused on analysing the experience gained during the period 1947. The major findings of the study were:

(i) After the imposition of imperial authority of India only those persons had access to bearing modern science who studied in English medium schools. During the British period vacillations uncertainty and aimless compromise were found both in making a school science policy and in its execution.

(ii) During the period of 1947-52 two views regarding teaching science were advocated. The syllabus for basic schools visualised the general science approach to teaching science at Elementary stage in an integrated way and not as a separate schools subject, while another view was to teach science as systematised knowledge according to the concept approach. The debate for having the same science curriculum for Rural and Urban schools also continued. The teaching of science was found to be not satisfactory, whatever, it was proposed to achieve could not be put into practice. One reason was inertia of the educational system.

(iii) The period 1952-57 was the period, when national efforts to improve secondary education were mounted. The Secondary Education Commission (1953) was against specialisation and recommended a general science course, i.e. a general introduction to all the broad and significant field of scientific knowledge, while at the same time it desired an understanding and appreciation of the fundamental principles of science. This ambiguity in policy decision was subjected to different interpretations at the implementation stage the national and state levels. Due to this the school science education policy appeared to be blended around from one idea to another and from one recommendation to another leading to vacillations in policy implementation.

(iv) During the period 1957-62, the major school science curricular trend was still general science. However, the echo of the concept approach could be heard in various seminars. This happened because of the absence of proper experimentation in the field of school science education for effective planning and implementation and a clear cut school science education policy could not emerge because of parallel and continuing viewpoints on school science, etc.

The major findings of the study of Mehna (1986) were:

(i) Six variables, viz. verbal intelligence, motivation for learning general science, scientific knowledge and aptitude, numerical ability, linking for teachers of science and interest in medicine were significant predictor of achievement of Class IX students in general science (R = 0.5773).

(ii) The significant predictor variables for achievement in physics for students of Class IX were the same as those found in the case at general science with the addition of one more variable abstract reasoning.

The research findings imply that the pupil's performance in science subjects can be improved: (a) If teachers succeed in generating a feeling of liking for them among pupils, (b) If teachers develop aptitude for science among children by providing scientific information, and (c) If teachers can motivate children to learn science subjects. This needs adequate training for teachers in making science teaching interesting and in training them in techniques of arousing pupil's motivation for learning science.

Following were the findings of the study of Khalwania (1986):

(i) The concept-based curriculum was more effective than the conventional curriculum in terms of acquisition of process skills as well as in developing better cognitive structure.

(ii) The students having high self-concept did not differ in process skill scores from students having low self-concept.

(iii) Levels of intelligence did not affect mean scores on the process skill test.

(iv) Intelligence acted as a redundant variables as far as development of cognitive structure was concerned.

(v) The high socio-economic status group and the low socio-economic groups did equally well in the acquisition of process skills in science.

(vi) Levels of self-concept did not affect the development of cognitive structures.

(vii) Curriculum types did not interact significantly with levels at intelligence, levels of self-concept and levels of socio-economic status.

(viii) The low socio-economic group following the concept-based curriculum scored significantly higher on process skills than the high self-concept and high socio-economic groups using the conventional curriculum.

(ix) The low ability students having low socio-economic status when taught the concept-based curriculum performed better on the cognitive structure test than high ability and high socio-economic group students.

(x) Students having high self-concept and high socio-economic status but taught through the conventional curriculum indicated low achievement.

(xi) Students with high self-concept and low socio-economic status differed significantly from students with high self-concept but low socio-economic status under the two types of curricula used in the study.

The findings of the study conducted by Lambhate (1987) were:

(i) The use of experimental instructional material by the teachers of the experimental group contributed towards the improvement of their performance.

(ii) The teachers of the experimental group performed better than those of the control group on: (a) Selection and organisation for contexts, (b) Use of proper scientific terminology, teaching aids and experimentation, and (c) Maintaining the class room discipline by sustaining the attention of students with the help of instructional materials.

(iii) The experimental instructional materials could not equip teachers to enable their pupils to think critically.

(iv) The effectiveness of the environment-based material in the teaching of science to Grade VI pupils in rural schools was demonstrated.

Malhotra (1988) in his study entitled "A Critical Study of the Existing Facilities of Science Teaching and Construction of Evaluation Instruments for its Supervision in Different Types of Secondary Schools in Delhi." He found that the three types of schools (Public, Government and Central) differed significantly in respect of existing facilities for science-based curricular and co-curricular activities. Supervision of theory classes as well as conferences and welfare of teachers and students.

Deshmukh (1991) studied Science education as a means of social change with special respect to health and hygienic habits found that lack of physical amenities, a loaded curriculum and failure to practice health habits latter on.

Singh (1993) studied teachers effectiveness in relation to their sex area and adjustment found that there was a significant difference between male and female teachers in their adjustment in favour of male teachers. The rural and urban teachers did not differs significantly in their adjustments.

Singh and Prabhat (1993) in their study on relationship between ego strength and job satisfaction, found ego strength and job satisfaction were significantly related. Male teachers had a higher level of correlation than their female counterparts. On their relationship male and female teachers did not differ significantly on their ego strength.

Padhi (1993) studied the home effects on pupils academic self-concept and achievement in Science, found that there was a significant correlation between Academic Self Concept (ASC), Achievement in Science (SC) and Home Environment (HE) dimension with a specific reference to control protectiveness, social isolation which were positive too. When high and low groups on the basis of ASC scores were compared it was found that two groups differed significantly on five HE dimensions. They include control, punishment, nurturance, rejection and permissiveness.

Thampurthy and Devi (1994) studied on interaction effect of creativity attitude towards problem-solving and social position on the achievement in Mathematics of Secondary School pupils. They found that positive substantial and significant relation existed between creativity and achievement in mathematics. Positive and high significant relation existed between attitude towards problem-solving and achievement in Mathematics. Positive moderate and significant relation existed between Socio-Economic Status (SES) and achievement in Mathematics.

Mohapatra (1995) studied on Development of Software package for teaching Chemistry to Class IX students of Madhya Pradesh state found that developed software package was found to be effective in terms of achievement of the students, on criterian tests seventy per cent of students achieved more than sixty per cent works. The developed software package was found significantly superior to traditional method. There was no significant difference in the male and female students towards development software package.

Rao (1995) in his study on teacher effectiveness in relation to creativity and interpersonal relationships found no significant relation between teacher effectiveness and the income or years of teaching experience of the teachers. Significant relations were found between teacher effectiveness, creativity and inter-personal relationship. Significant relations were found between rural and urban teachers with reference to inter-personal relationships.

Rali (1995) in his study of the awareness and attitude of teachers and students of high schools towards environmental education in Jabalpur District found that the students and teachers differed significantly on their environmental knowledge in favour of teaching. Urban teachers and rural teachers differed significantly on their awareness of environmental problems.

2.4 STUDIES AT THE STATE LEVEL

Trend of Research in Science Education at the State Level

In Orissa, after Independence, it is difficult to find much related studies in the field of Science Education. At the initial stage there were no much coordinated efforts to bring out the problems faced by the teachers and the students in the area of science teaching and clearing. Even science was not considered as an important subject in school curriculum. At the beginning the science teaching was confined to middle school and high school level. The contents were very much rudimentary. Gradually, this area was influenced by the research findings done in outside the State. Science in the form of general science occupied a space even in primary school curriculum and now under the caption of Environmental Studies from the beginning of schooling. The contents lost its traditionality and now it seems, it is quite upto-date. The Board of Secondary Education, Orissa and SCERT. Orissa put co-ordinated efforts to elevate in the status of science as a subject in school curriculum both in Elementary Level and Secondary Level. Their efforts to elevate in the status level and secondary level. Their effort is very much based on the results of the research findings available in the State and outside the State and in national framework of science curriculum. Mostly the researches done in the state were at PG level. Rare researches were found at Doctoral level. Some of the researches were worth mentioning here as they were found quite relevant.

A five year project entitled "Teaching Science Scientifically in the High Schools of Orissa" sponsored by the Ministry of Education, Government of India (1959) was undertaken at Radhanth Training College, Cuttack during the period 1954-59.

The project covered the following aspects under the guidance of Dr. R.C. Dash (Mohanty, 1987):

(a) Survey of the current practices in teaching science in the High Schools of Orissa with the help of questionnaire sent to the teachers in respect of the objectives, methods, curriculum, laboratory and library facilities, the teaching aids and examination.
(b) Study of pupil's interest in science with the help questionnaire given to the pupils.
(c) Analysis of man's activities, way of living and the environment in which he lives to determine the scientific knowledge acquired in life.
(d) Analysis of General Science syllabi and standard text-books of different States in General Science and its suitability for High Schools of Orissa in the light of the finding of study.
(e) Formulation of a new method of teaching in General Science and its experimental try out and evaluation.

The State level study on the Science education had great importance to evolve a dynamic curriculum for secondary school children. Initially little importance was given on Science as a subject in School. Board of Secondary Education and SCERT put co-ordinated effort to elevate the status of science as a subject in school curriculum both in elementary and secondary level. In 1954-59 during the period the project under the guidance of Dr. R.C. Dash entitled "Teaching Science Scientifically in the High Schools of Orissa". The overall status and standard of Science Education was examined and recommended for the further improvement.

Mishra (1977) studied the efficacy of inquiry teaching for developing Scientific concepts over the traditional method of teaching. Pradhan (1978) evaluated the different aspects of the text-book rating its suitability and recommended for its improvement. Mishra (1980) examined the curricular validity of examination in general science conducted by Board of Secondary Education, Orissa.

Behera (1981) conducted an evaluation of text in Science with reference to different objectives. Jena (1982) investigated into the problem of science teachers and science teaching and library, laboratory status in secondary school.

Rout (1982) assessed the quality of instruction imparted in our schools and to find out the various instructional facilities available. He reviewed the relationship between instruction and achievement. Dash (1983) assessed the attitude of girl students towards science teaching. He found that girl students had favourable attitude towards Science Education.

Mishra (1985) studied the attitude of secondary school students towards science. Sarangi (1983) presented the status of school Science Education in Orissa in the historical perspective with an objective to improve it.

Tripathy (1986) examined the problems of science teachers and physical facilities for Science Education. Mohanty (1987) examined the problems of science teaching and improve the status of Science Education through improvement of laboratory, library and other physical facilities.

Mishra (1987) examined the system of examination and importance of objective type achievement test. Also attitude of girls towards Science Education was studied by him.

Haque (1987) evaluated the importance of open book test and achievement in Science Education. Mishra (1990) studied the status of Science teaching in Secondary Schools.

Behera (1992) analysed the different aspects of science curriculum and recommended for the enrichment of science education through instructional objectives. Naik (1993) discussed staffing pattern and teacher requirements to man the schools and improvement of library and laboratory condition for Science Education.

Some individual studies with their objectives and findings are given here to have a clear picture of the status of Science Education in the state of Orissa.

Mishra (1977) study on the efficacy of enquiry teaching for developing scientific concepts over traditional methods of teaching science was undertaken as a tryout for improving the performance of pupils and developing scientific concept in them as a sample study. The experimental study was done and the investigator concluded that enquiry approach of teaching science was better than the traditional methods for the development of scientific concepts.

The main objective of the study conducted by Pradhan (1978) were to review the different aspects of the text-book for rating their suitability and to recommend for their improvement. The author to the physics part of the Classes IX, X and XI only. The major findings obtained were as follows:

- The physical aspects were slightly fair.
- Syllabus, content organisation, language, teaching and learning were fair.
- Exercise in the aspects like (a) Interest in the aspects like, (b) Reserving, (c) Judgement, (d) Numerical questions were poor.
- There was no provision for teacher's manual.
- Objectives of science curriculum and content were developed poorly.

The study of Mishra (1980) revealed the following findings after studying curricular validity and reliability of public examination in general science:

- The average marks of boys were more than that of girls.
- The co-efficient of correlation between Board marks and school marks of boys was 0.70 and that of girls was 0.51.
- Both were significant at 0.01 level of significance.
- There was significant relationship between School marks and Board marks.

Behera (1981) conducted an evaluation of text-book in Science. In this study few objectives were taken viz. to find out the limitations of the said text-book for High School to offer suggestion on the basis of finding. To enlighten the teachers about the quality of a good text book. Out of this study 16 aspects of the book were considered to be improved. In the light of the findings it was recommended as many as suggestions for the qualitative improvement.

Jena (1982) undertook the study entitled "A Study of Relationship between Instruction and Achievement in General Science in the High Schools of Sambalpur Town" and found that a low co-relation existed between achievement and nature of organisation. A substantial positive co-relation between laboratory and achievement. The difference between mean achievement scores of well-equipped High Schools and poorly equipped High Schools was significant. The schools having better instructional facilities obviously showed better results in science.

The main objectives of the study conducted by Dash (1983) was to find out the attitude of girl students towards science teaching. The main findings of the study was that the girl students had favourable attitude towards science teaching and learning.

Findings of the study conducted by Mishra (1985) were:

- Training developed a positive attitude in boys and girls.
- Validity and reliability co-efficient of the test was found to be significant. The test was highly valid and reliable.

In his comparative study of Science Education, Sarangi (1983) presented the status of school Science Education in Orissa in the historical perspective with the objective of improving it to a desirable standard. The major findings of the study were:

- The trends so identified indicated that Science Education which existed in ancient and medieval Orissa continued with ups and down till its revival during the British period.
- It has taken rapid stride during the early years of Independence.
- The cultural traditions of Orissa, ignorance of the poverty-striken people were mainly responsible for low level of Science Education in the past.

The major findings of the study of Tripathy (1986) indicated that:

(1) About 37.5 per cent of schools had only science teachers. There were no sufficient class rooms in 60 per cent of schools, some facilities were provided in 92.5 per cent of the schools but these were quite inadequate. Almost all schools had no science laboratory.

(2) Due to lack of funds, interest of science teachers the science teaching could not succeed.

The major findings of the doctoral study conducted by Mohanty (1987) are:

- The Board of Secondary Education, Orissa should appoint more than one expert in science to look to the improvement of science teaching in the State to meet the challenges arising out of large number of secondary schools.
- As regards the equipments and laboratory facilities all the schools were deficient.

- All the teachers follow the demonstration-*cum*-discussion method for teaching science which is most suitable in our condition.

The major objective of the study undertaken by Mishra (1987) was to assess the attitude of girl students of secondary schools towards science. The findings of the study revealed that there was high significant difference between the attitude of low achievers and higher achievers towards science.

The findings of the study conducted Haque (1987) indicated that:

- Open book tests in science had measured, what the traditional science test measured.
- The students performance in both forms of the open book test was very low in view of the maximum possible score.
- There was high relationship between the scores on both forms of the open book test.

The main objective of the study conducted by Mishra (1990) was to critically appraise the science teaching in secondary schools. The analysis of the data showed that:

- About 72.5 per cent of schools had no adequate science teachers.
- Only 20 per cent of schools had special science class-room and 27.5 per cent of schools only had charts in science laboratories.
- As many as 97.5 per cent of schools were sincere to give home assignments to students.
- Only 4.5 per cent of schools were financed properly.
- Science experts of Board of Secondary Education (BSE) Orissa visited schools occasionally.

The major findings of the study undertaken by Behera (1992) were:

- The contents included in the physical science text-books were upto-date and in accordance with the syllabus. There was enrichment materials for brighter students.
- Instructional objectives had not been properly indicated in the text-book.
- Clarity of the content was not ensured.

- The contents were in conformity with the objectives of higher education.
- The contents were not interesting to the learner.
- The contents were useful to the teachers.
- Contents did not match the mental level of the students.
- The content had no practical value to real life situations.
- Experimentation and laboratory work had not been given due importance. The book has been more theoretical.
- The explanation of content was not lively.
- Various types of questions had been given in exercises.
- Questions had not been proportionately distributed among the instructional objectives.
- Application aspect of the book was not satisfactory.
- Examples used in the book were not adequate and clear.

The findings of the study conducted by Naik (1993) were:

- About 37.5 per cent of the schools had only one science teachers and 42.5 per cent of the schools had two science teachers. Due to limited number of science teachers their work-load seemed to be very heavy for them. They were teaching other subject besides science and did no get extra time to involve themselves in other science-based activities.
- It was found that due to poor financial condition most of the schools were not provided with well furnished laboratories, buildings, science rooms, etc. for the students.
- Library facility was provided in 92.5 per cent of the schools. But sufficient science books and journals were present in 30 per cent of schools only. The number and type of reference books were very few.
- All most all the schools had no laboratories for students. Teaching aids such as Charts, Models and Diagrams, etc. were available in 45 per cent of the schools as main teaching aids.
- Majority of the teachers were not satisfied with the present time table due to heavy work load.
- Maximum schools could not conduct different science-based activities due to lack of funds which has been mentioned.
- It was found that assessment of the pupils achievement was done through the class-work, home-work and different periodical examinations.

- The financial position in all the schools were not sound generally science teaching needs laboratories and more teaching aids than any other subject. These needs could not be fulfilled without financial help.
- Science education should primarily be concerned with the education of mind and it should consist in identification of mental abilities and way and means to develop those among younger generation. The researches in Science Education as revealed bear different connotation and those researches were in environmental education, science curriculum and text-book, evaluation of scientific attitude and interest, creativity in science, construction of test in science. Correlated achievement of the students in science analysis of Science Education researches clearly indicated the need for identification of certain priority areas, which contributed significantly to the present day society. These would have created through the development of various innovative curricula in science and allied discipline. The efforts must directed to the generation of knowledge concerned with learning science and instruction to the people.

The present vision of education in science is that science and technology should sufficiently correlated to the real life situation of a student. The science education programmes should be developed in harmony with modern condition of science, technology and society. The present day research should help to establish coherent relationship in between those components.

3

Science Education Programme: Methodology

3.1 INTRODUCTION

A research work can only be successful if an appropriate method is adopted. Method always occupies an important place in a study. It is the way of investigation into the problem. An ideal method is adopted to make this study systematic and satisfactory. The result would be ambiguous and confusing if the method of study is not appropriate. Hence, there is a need to narrate and evaluate the methods used in the investigation.

The primary task is to collect the relevant information from different sources such as secondary school teachers who teach science, experts in science education who are responsible for developing the curriculum and its transaction. The survey type methodology was thought to be most suitable to be adopted in this study. Different tools such as questionnaires, interview schedule and opinionnaire were developed to collect the necessary information from different relevant sources.

3.2 SAMPLE

The data were collected on the basis of a proper sampling. The technique of stratified random sampling was adopted for the purpose. The sample thus selected was systematic representation of all the secondary schools of Orissa. Fifty-one schools have been selected randomly which are affiliated to the Board of Secondary Education (BSE), Cuttack, Orissa and twelve schools from Central Board of Secondary Education (CBSE) pattern to know the global problems involved in science teaching at secondary level. In the sample all the English Medium Schools were affiliated to CBSE, New Delhi. The sample schools belonged to different categories such as Government and non-Government, English and Oriya medium of instructions, urban and rural. Out of 5232 secondary schools affiliated to BSE, Orissa, 51 were selected from nine districts, out of which 33 were Government and eighteen were non-Government. Twenty schools were situated in rural area, and 31 schools in urban places. Out of 20 rural schools five were Boys' Schools and fifteen were Co-education Schools, whereas from among the 31 urban schools 9 were Boys' Schools, 6 Girls' Schools and 16 were Co-education type. All the CBSE affiliated schools were co-educational and situated in urban areas. It is meant for those who can afford to pay for their children's education. These schools are basically English Medium Institutions. But in all the BSE schools Oriya was the medium of instruction and students hail from a wide cross-section of the society. Figure 3.1 indicates the distribution of sample schools.

Fig. 3.1: Showing Distribution of Sample Schools

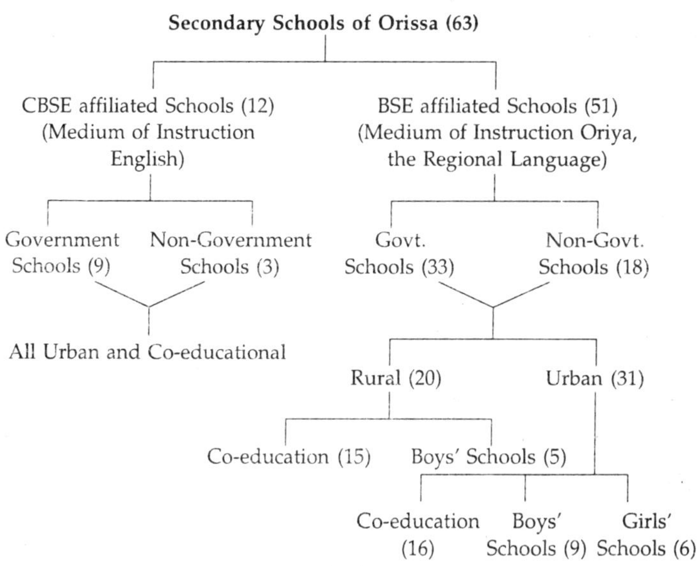

The schools are selected from nine districts of Orissa, out of total 30 districts and those were; Balasore, Bolangir, Bargarh, Cuttack, Ganjam, Khurda, Puri, Sundargarh and Sambalpur.

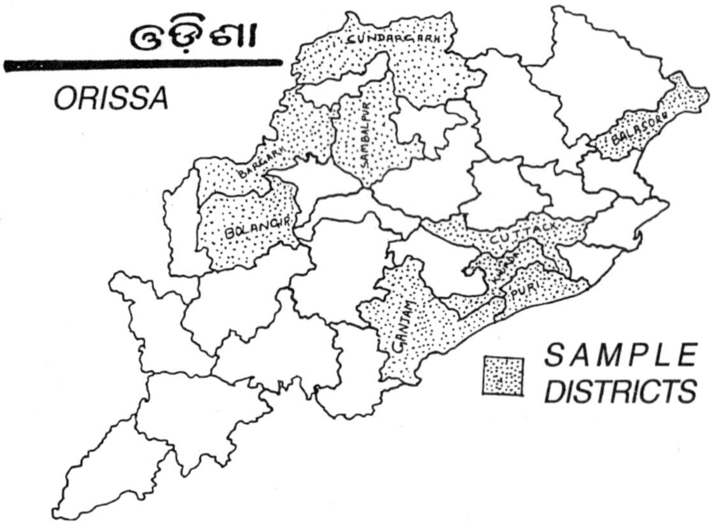

TABLE 3.1
Distribution of Sample Schools (District and Agency-wise)

	CBSE		*BSE*	
	Govt.	*Non-Govt.*	*Govt.*	*Non-Govt.*
1. Balasore	1	—	4	2
2. Bolangir	1	—	3	2
3. Cuttack	1	—	5	1
4. Khurda	1	—	3	3
5. Puri	4	3	4	2
6. Sambalpur	1	—	4	2
7. Bargarh	–	—	3	2
8. Ganjam	–	—	4	2
9. Sundargarh	–	—	3	2
Total	9 +	3 = 12	33 +	18 = 51

Data were collected from different personnel like heads of the schools, science teachers, students of higher classes of the schools, science supervisors working in the office of the circle inspector of schools and educationists who were concerned about science education. Altogether 63 headmasters, 230 science teachers (180 from BSE and 50 from CBSE), 500 students (400 from BSE and 100 from CBSE affiliated schools), 15 science supervisors and experts and 15 educationists constituted the sample.

3.3 PILOT STUDY

The results of secondary schools at the final examinations affiliated to BSE, Orissa are far from satisfaction in general. It is observed that particularly the achievements of students in the subjects like English, Mathematics and General Science exhibit a very poor show, in State schools in a large scale and in CBSE affiliated schools in a minor scale. The informal survey of the condition of schools supported this view also. To get a concrete idea of this problem, it was decided to have personal visit to some urban and rural schools of different categories such as BSE affiliated and CBSE affiliated schools of Boys, Girls, and Co-education schools. The Headmasters and science teachers were brought to the discussion. Some informal discussion was conducted with parents also. The advantage was taken of being a working science teacher and the informal facts available from different sources revealed that there existed some serious problems in science curriculum and in transactional strategies.

3.4 INSTRUMENTATION

Utmost care was taken for construction of different tools to gather data from multiple sources. Questionnaire and opinionnaire are common tools generally used to collect data on different issues from various angles from the primary sources. These consist of a bunch of items basically objective and restricted answer type and some are open ended in nature. Questionnaires were developed to elicit the remarks and information from Headmasters, Science teachers and students of Secondary Schools affiliated to both BSE and CBSE. Opinionnaire was developed to gather the views and suggestions of educational experts and administrators. Interview schedule was developed for educationists to collect their views on particular issues of science education in secondary schools of Orissa.

3.5 PREPARATION OF TOOLS

Preparation of tools is a task of great importance for collecting data. Reliability and validity of such tools are to be given due importance at the time of their preparation. These draft tools were prepared with due consultation with educational experts, administrators and experienced teachers. Hundreds of items were developed to be included in the questionnaires, opinionnaires and interview schedule. After preparation tools, those were sent to a panel of experts for their opinion. They took their own time to provide necessary suggestion on each tool. The suggestions were then discussed with the experts and final drafts were prepared after the inclusion of necessary modifications in each tool on the basis of its clarity, objectivity, usability reliability and validity.

3.5.1 Questionnaire for Headmaster

A questionnaire was prepared for the sample Headmasters (51 BSE and 12 CBSE) with great care. It tried to seek general information about the individual school, the instructional facilities for teaching science, infrastructural facilities available for it, regarding the management and utilization of facilities, co-curricular activities usually conducted, information regarding the finance, supervision and inspection system, time table, course content and methodology to know the status and relevance of science education in the sample schools. Scope was provided at the end of the tool to enlist suggestions and criticism about the existing science curriculum by the head of institution.

3.5.2 Questionnaire for Science Teacher

The questionnaire was developed to elicit information from the science teachers of secondary schools of Orissa. The first section of it is meant for eliciting information as regards the status of science education in secondary schools, whereas the second part reveals specific information as regards the problems faced by science teachers in the schools in the teaching process.

The sample science teachers (180 BSE and 50 CBSE) were contacted first hand for their thoughtful views and remarks through the questionnaire. The section 'A' of the questionnaire consists of nine broad areas and each area carries five to seven items. The areas were general information about the locality, type, nature and management of the school, the staff position and views of teachers on the adequacy of their number, the number of periods allotted weekly for teaching the subject. Queries were made as regards the science room facilities, i.e. demonstration table, black-board, charts, maps, etc. including the electric and water supply. Science laboratory and library are important components of school, some items also dealt with to reveal information about those facilities. Items on teaching aid facilities included to know the details about the other facilities, i.e. Botanical garden, Science Club, etc. and to elicit the views of science teachers on management of co-curricular activities in science. Some queries were made on the assignments given to the students, time table, evaluation and remarks on course content, method of teaching and standard of text-books. The teachers were also asked regarding the availability of science journals and magazines in the school. The teachers were requested to give their suggestions for the improvement of science education programme.

The section 'B' of the questionnaire consists of eight broad problem areas such as problems related to availability of in-service training programme, administration, laboratory facilities, instructional materials, class room situation, methodology of teaching, organisation of co-curricular activities and evaluation, etc. There are fifty items pertaining to the above mentioned broad areas. Through this section of the questionnaire an attempt was made to locate the problems of science education from different angles.

3.5.3 Questionnaire for the Students (CBSE and BSE)

A questionnaire was prepared for both CBSE and BSE affiliated secondary school students both in English and Oriya language. Questionnaires were given to 400 BSE and 100 CBSE school students. Students were asked to respond to the questions pertaining to general information such as locality of the school and about the science teachers and their attitude towards students, method of teaching, use of aids, field trips, completion of course in time, etc. Information in relation to science room facilities, black boards, electric connections, gas facilities, science library and laboratory facilities were collected by the help of questionnaire also. Queries on co-curricular activities like study tour, field study, etc. participation in science exhibition programmes, competition and other activities and participation in inter-school competitions were ascertained through different items. Data pertaining to assignments, time-table allotment, course-content and text books also collected with the help of the items included in the questionnaire.

3.5.4 Opinionnaire for Science Supervisors and Experts

Fifteen science supervisors and experts responded to the opinionnaire. The items were framed to elicit the opinions pertaining to the facilities available in secondary schools for science education. Suggestions were elicited for improving the present position, planning and management of co-curricular activities in science, etc. Sufficient care was taken to elicit suggestions for improving present evaluation system in science education, inspection and supervision of science programmes conducted in schools and other areas through this opinionnaire.

3.5.5 Interview Schedule for Educationists

Fifteen educationists were interviewed on the areas such as syllabus improvement, methods of teaching, physical facilities available for practical and co-curricular activities inspection for improving science education programme etc.

3.6 ADMINISTRATION OF TOOLS

The tools thus prepared were administered on the target groups. The Science Teachers, Headmasters and the Students were personally contacted to collect their responses. Only in few cases, the help was sought from postal system.

An instruction sheet was attached to each questionnaire to ensure clear understanding by the target group. Through individual meetings with the respondents, proper rapport was established and assurance was given about the confidentiality of their responses. They were sufficiently motivated to act upon for the assigned work and were provided sufficient time to give their responses in the tools provided. All together 63 Headmasters, 230 Science Teachers and 500 Students responded with valuable information.

The opinionnaire and the interview schedule were administered in similar way. Fifteen Science Supervisors and Experts related to teaching science gave their expert opinion which were quite useful for this study. Fifteen Educationists were interviewed and their views were recorded for the study.

4

Analysis of Science Education Programme

4.1 INFORMATION PROVIDED BY THE HEADMASTERS

4.1.1 Demographic Status of the Sample Schools

It is revealed from the data supplied by the Headmasters of sample institutions that 4.77 percent High Schools were developed prior to 1900 A.D. and 14.28 percent schools established prior to independence, i.e. between 1900 A.D. to 1947 A.D. while 80.95 percent sample schools started functioning after independence. The disparity as regards facilities available in urban and rural areas were quite conspicuous. The data collected from the sample schools indicated that 31.74 percent schools located in rural area and rest of the schools are situated in urban area.

The number of Co-education schools were more than Boys' or Girls' High Schools. It was found that 68.25 percent sample schools were co-educational while the number of Boys' Schools were more than the Girls' Schools. It was found that in Orissa few secondary schools were affiliated to Central Board of Secondary Education (CBSE), New Delhi and quite a majority were affiliated to Board of Secondary Education (BSE), Orissa. Out of sample CBSE schools only 25 percent schools were managed by Private Organisations and rest of the schools were Government managed. But in BSE schools 64.70 percent schools were Government institutions while rest of the schools were run by Private Bodies.

The difference in enrolment between boys and girls were quite distinct. The data showed that boys were 30 percent more than the girls in number. The classes were divided into sections on the basis of the students' strength in a particular class. In BSE schools a class could be divided into two sections, if the number of students exceeds fifty, while the number of students were restricted to forty in CBSE affiliated schools. For the qualitative education the teacher-pupil ratio must be 1:40 in BSE schools and 1:35 in CBSE schools. But this theory is different from practice continuing in BSE schools. In many schools several teaching posts were remained vacant for years together while CBSE schools were above such problems.

4.1.2 Condition for Transacting Science Curriculum

Science is one of the important subjects in secondary school stage. Usually science subject is transacted by two sets of teachers' namely physical science group teachers who are supposed to teach Mathematics, Physics and Chemistry while natural science teachers in charge of teaching Biology portion of science course. The number of science teachers increases in accordance with the opening of new sections. In BSE schools the situation was precarious as the practice differs from theory. In many cases the number of teachers are not commensurated with the work load of sections and in several schools science subject was taught by under qualified and untrained teachers. It was found that 42.20 percent science teachers were women. Among the Physical Science teachers the percentage of male teachers were more (61.82 percent) while the females were engaged (58.63 percentage) in teaching Biological Sciences.

As science is a practical subject it requires the presence of auxiliary staff such as laboratory assistants and attendants. It was found that in 92 percent schools the work of laboratory assistants were carried out by the science teachers themselves and the work of attendants done by the school peon, in some cases even by the teachers themselves. As per data 80 percent CBSE schools have laboratory assistants and in 3 percent of old BSE schools have attendants post only. As stated earlier the BSE affiliated schools faced the problem of inadequacy of teachers and other staff. Some teachers teach science although they were originally not from science discipline. About 83.33 percent of CBSE schools and 74.50 percent BSE schools had required number of science teachers to teach the subject. As the Head of institutions opined the teachers were not able to meet the needs of classes because of the following reasons:

- Classes were over-crowded.

- Teachers did not get salary in time and even it was inadequate in private managed schools.
- Teachers were preoccupied by the problem arising out of the place of their posting.
- A sizeable number of students belonged to low average group.
- Non-availability of required teaching aids and other transactional facilities.

Further the Head of the institutions were of the opinion that most of their teachers so far had not undergone any in-service training programmes for teaching science. A few teachers only could avail the chance of undergoing some specific in-service training programmes conducted by Board of Secondary Education (BSE), Central Boards of Secondary Education (CBSE), Kendriya Vidyalaya Sangathan (KVS), State Council of Educational Research and Training (SCERT) and National Council of Educational Research and Training (NCERT). The programmes attended by the teachers were orientation courses in content and methodology, workshop leading to development of teachers' handbook and students' workbook, etc. But these facilities could not be available to about 75.80 percent teachers serving in BSE schools and 48.80 percent teachers of CBSE affiliated schools.

It was found that 32 percent science teachers were used to take extra classes to complete the science course while 30 percent teachers usually engaged in private tuition to help the students particularly in physical science portion. As tuition was sought by majority of parents to provide additional help to their children it became a necessity all over Orissa irrespective of Urban and Rural set-up now. Hence, the class-room teaching might not be that effective for the students as expected.

Most of the Headmasters (78.90 percent) did not favour tuition but some favoured it because of the following reasons:

- Non-availability of sufficient time for teaching during school hour as science teaching requires more time for conceptual clarity.
- Least scope for providing individual attention to the students in over-crowded classes.
- Less scope for correcting home tasks in large class room set-up.

- Some times parents compel teachers to undertake private tuition.
- Frequent practice of some difficult content matter is possible in tuition classes but not in class room set-up.
- Ten to twelve students can be undertaken in one batch of tuition class, which makes teaching and learning more effective.

Government does not allow teachers to be engaged in private tuition. Central Government has strictly prohibited private tuition practices in Government schools. To discourage teachers of getting involved in private tuitions every teacher is being given a teaching allowance of Rs. 100 per month. But in the revised new pay scale this provision is not reflected. This facility was not extended by the Government of Orissa. Rather State Government frequently instructs the Headmasters to prevent private tuition practices among the teachers. But some times because of certain specific problems Head of the institutions recommended the parents to send their children either for coaching classes conducted by the school in out of school hours or to send their children to some good teachers for private tuition. The specific problems of recommending for private tuition cited by Heads of the institution are:

- Parents many times approach teachers or Headmasters for private tuition.
- To get good result of the school in public examinations Headmasters allow some good teachers to take some special care of the students.
- Specially science teachers were recommended for private tuitions as the difficulty level of the subject is more than some other subjects as viewed by the Heads.

4.1.3 Infrastructural Facilities Available in Institution

Science teaching occupies a crucial importance as it has practical experiment to demonstrate experiments to students at the time of need. To satisfy the students' requirements, essential materials and more time are required. It was widely felt from the facts collected that the consumable chemicals those were available in laboratory could fulfil 40 percent of its requirement. The laboratory facilities were not available even in 96.07 percent BSE schools while 66.65 percent of CBSE schools had laboratories of average condition. The equipments were available in 41.17 percent schools in BSE affiliated schools although laboratory facilities could not be made available. These equipments were stored in other rooms not meant for science laboratory. But the CBSE affiliated schools have such facilities in 66.65 percent cases. The teaching aids were not adequately available in 65 percent schools to teach science. In many cases the teachers were not used to take teaching aids to the classes as the school had no such materials to be used. There are several shortcomings in the laboratory as revealed or the sample Headmasters. Those are:

- Lack of funds to renovate the condition, i.e. equipment, building and chemicals.
- Inadequate number of non-teaching staff, i.e. laboratory assistants and attendants.
- Insufficient consumable chemicals and materials.
- Inadequate space in the laboratory.
- Lack of interest of the management to provide such facilities.
- Improper ventilation in the laboratory.
- No proper planning for laboratory construction.

4.1.4 Management and Utilisation of Facilities

As it has already been mentioned that the science teachers were quite capable of using teaching aids but because of non-availability of such materials in schools they became helpless. Some of the ambitious teachers (30 percent) used to make use of aids of low cost and no cost while teaching science. But Majority (70 percent) teachers tried to teach with least aids and often without teaching aids. Another very important fact was revealed from the Headmasters that only 32 percent teachers found it difficult to complete the course because of the extensive use of teaching aids. The CBSE sample schools took utmost care to use teaching aids but about 23 percent of such schools faced difficulty as regards the availability of aids.

4.1.5 Co-curricular Activities

Co-curricular activities are integral part of curricular activities. Former is supplementary to latter without which learning is incomplete. Different types of co-curricular activities are conducted at secondary level. Science exhibition is one of those activities. It is being conducted in different schools and provide scope for participation of students in it at different levels such as Circle, State and National. But schools has to play an important role in it. In Orissa, Circle level, State level science exhibitions and competitions are organised. Birla Industrial Technical Museum (BITM), Calcutta, Eastern India Science Camp are organised annually. NCERT conducts Jawaharlal Nehru, National level Science Exhibition on rotation in different States for children annually. Some enthusiastic schools encourage their students to participate in such activities. Even BITM, Calcutta and Science Museum, Bhubaneswar organise mobile science exhibition at different places on request. It was found that only 30 percent teachers in BSE schools encouraged students to participate in exhibition and other science activities. In CBSE schools 69.60 percent teachers tried to expose their students through such co-curricular activities, i.e. exhibition and different kinds of competitions. Only 19.04 percent schools organised exhibition bi-annually while 39.68 percent schools organised it annually and Science Museum is a distant dream in most of the schools. Science equipments were just stored in almirahs which were never or seldom used. Science Club activities were carried out just in papers. It was found that 43.13 percent BSE schools and 91.66 percent CBSE schools sent their student representative to inter-school competitions in Debate, Essay, Eloquency, Quiz, etc. A few schools had some highly ambitious teachers who could undertake programmes through science club activities to review different causes and consequences of problems related to ecology, energy pollution, poverty, etc.

As revealed from the opinion of the Head of institutions that 54.90 percent of BSE schools 33.33 percent CBSE schools participated through student representatives in inter-school competitions related to science quiz, essay competitions and debate competitions at the district level. The total picture of the participation of BSE and CBSE schools are well-illustrated in the following graphic representations in different levels (Distt. Circle, State and National).

From the following graphics it was quite clear that as the passing of the time the participation of both BSE and CBSE schools

Fig. 4.1: Graphic presentation of Co-curricular activities i.e., Debate, Quiz and Science Exhibition at different levels, viz. Circles, State and National Level

DEBATE COMPETITION

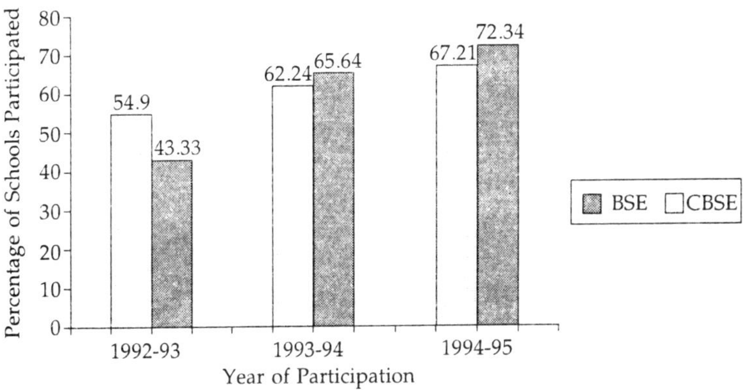

QUIZ COMPETITION

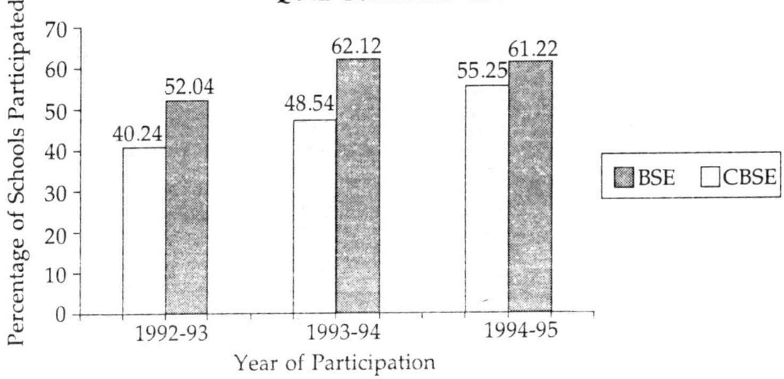

SCIENCE EXHIBITION

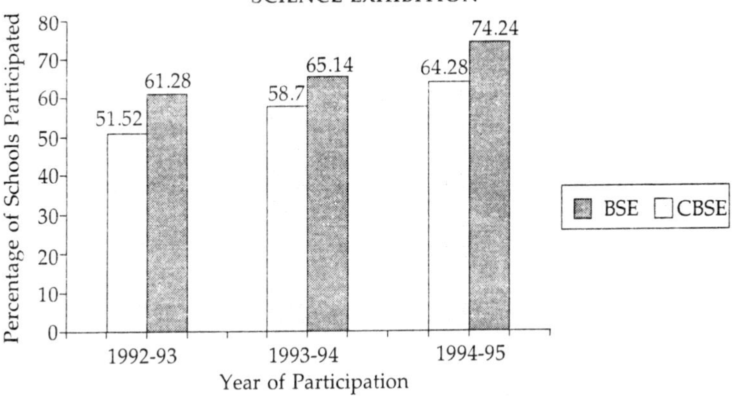

were in increasing order in all the fields of co-curricular activities mentioned above. It is also observed that CBSE participants were more in compare to their counter-parts in BSE schools.

4.1.6 Finance

Government grants for both infrastructural and instructional for teaching science is highly essential. But 76.19 percent schools could not receive any grant while other schools received a scanty grant which was not adequate to meet the requirements. Only 3.17 percent of sample schools collected money from students and others occasionally for improvement of science laboratory and materials for teaching science. Although allocation of more money for science teaching is widely felt yet it suffered from sheer negligence. Indifferent attitude of authority made the situation worst. There was neither public donation nor the schools were empowered to collect fund from other sources officially. The funds allocated to the schools were only for maintenance which was quite insufficient for processing and sustenance of work.

As indicated earlier fund is essential for infrastructural and instructional purposes of teaching science, likewise some fund is also essential for conducting some co-curricular activities related to science teaching. Mostly those activities were conducted in some sample schools through collection of fees from students. To put forth the examples of such activities few schools conducted science exhibition, field-trips organised to observe flora and fauna of different areas, visit to science museum and some industrial area, conducting and attending state level, circle level science quiz, debate competition and some other similar activities, preparing and exhibiting graphic teaching aids and project work by the students, some specific experiment and demonstration of some particular activities. No sample school received any grant from any source to conduct such activities. Mostly they were dependent on their students' resource in this regard non-officially. The BSE affiliated schools very rarely conducted such activities but 50 percent CBSE schools conduct such activities through the means as discussed.

4.1.7 Inspection

Inspection means critical examination of one or more aspects of the school and its programmes. Historically speaking it was introduced in the education system to enforce control and authority as an executive arm of the Government. The officers in charge of inspection were mainly educational administrative officials who used to pay visit to schools with a view to checking the work of teachers and progress of pupils as per the rules and standards prescribed by the Government from time to time. It ensures the improvement of teaching standard and provide remedial measures to over come the problem. But unfortunately inspection in present set-up has suffered from ailments which needs immediate panacea measures to control the situation and keep up the standard and status of teaching in general and science teaching in particular. As reported 25 percent BSE schools were visited by science experts from BSE, Orissa, Cuttack. The Board of Secondary Education, Orissa has appointed subject experts in science for enrichment of academic activities in teaching science. Government CBSE schools were supervised by inspecting team formed by their authorities. But the private managed CBSE schools were deprived of the services of such subject experts. Only 45 percent BSE schools were supervised by Inspectors of Schools that too once in an academic year. Their visit played no role in improvement of academic atmosphere of the school. It was also found that 35 percent sample schools were visited by some kind of science experts. But the overall supervision was not satisfactory as most of the problems were overlooked or unchanged for years together. Headmaster has got specific role in inspection and supervision of classes. About 25 percent of Headmasters in BSE schools undertook class inspection work occasionally but CBSE school Headmasters engaged themselves in regular class inspection work, it created serious problem as regards to regular academic inspection of science classes when Head of the institution did not have science background. Many BSE and CBSE schools suffered from this kind of problem.

4.1.8 Time-Table

Time-table is an important aspect of class room teaching. About 87 percent sample schools' science teachers were satisfied with the number of classes available for transaction and 85 percent teachers completed the course in due time as opined by Headmasters. Even some teachers (30 percent) use to take extra classes to complete the course. It seems in almost all BSE schools a science teacher has been assigned with 32 periods in average in a week to teach science while in CBSE schools, one teacher has to take 18 classes per week in which one has to engage the learner in curricular and co-curricular activities.

But as opined by the Head of institutions it was revealed that there was no availability of periods for conducting every specific co-curricular activity during regular class work. Most of the co-curricular activity, if at all conducted were taken up beyond class hours. Mostly the laboratory work in CBSE schools found some place in day-to-day classes. But in BSE schools no such provision was available. Now, it was very clear from the fact that the periods were mostly used for monotonous curricular activities where teacher had to exhibit his/her competencies in dealing the subject mostly theoretically. Practical work was very much neglected in the time-table of the schools.

4.1.9 Course Content and Methodology

Course content and methodology occupies an important place in curricular transaction. It is known that curricular materials are the tasks or events related directly to the contents prescribed in syllabus. Method of transaction is the way to achieve the curricular goal. Science course is changing from time to time to adhere update innovations and development in the field of different branches of science. The syllabus being packed with important and useful material as assessed by 87 percent Headmasters while 13 percent of them sought change in the course.

Methods of teaching plays a key role to transact course. Teachers have been provided with full autonomy as regards the use of teaching strategies, approaches and designs. They are supposed to evolve their unique strategies to deal effectively with the exigencies they faced during transactional period. Science is a practical-oriented process-based subject. It needs upto-date flexible methodologies. But to our great disappointment about 40 percent Headmasters had expressed their dissatisfaction as regards methodology adopted by their teachers. Teachers just adopted text book and lecture method which made science teaching and learning monotonous and difficult. While 58.73 percent sample school Headmasters expressed their satisfaction on the methods adopted by their teachers. Time to time meetings were conducted by the Headmasters (60 percent) to ensure better teaching and promote sincerity with teachers. It was found that about 72 percent Headmasters of sample schools were satisfied with the performance of the science teachers working with them.

Headmasters suggested a great deal to bring infrastructural change to ensure better laboratory, special library, better science room facilities and adequate financial sanction for purchase of both consumable and other equipment for laboratory. They have expressed concern over the existing provision of supervision and improvement of science education. Science Club, Eco Club and Botanical gardens are also of high importance for which fund and place should be provided to give a new direction to science teaching in our State. The above analysis revealed that above all science teaching condition is deplorable in our state. Necessary attempts should be made at different quarters of the society for the improvement of science teaching as opined by the Heads of sample institutions.

4.2 INFORMATION PROVIDED BY THE SCIENCE TEACHERS

4.2.1 General Information about the Sample School

In relation to the demographic status of the institutions it was previously made clear that 31.74 percent schools were located in rural areas and rest of the schools were situated in urban areas of Orissa. It was found that 68.25 percent of the sample schools were Co-educational and number of Boys' schools were more than Girls' schools. About 25 percent of CBSE affiliated schools were managed by private bodies while rest of the same schools were government managed. Likewise 64.70 percent BSE affiliated schools were managed by government and rest of the sample schools run by private bodies. The overall picture of management of secondary education in Orissa indicated that majority of schools were managed by Government. Altogether 230 science teachers out of which 180 teachers from BSE and 50 teachers from CBSE schools were included in the sample for the purpose of collecting information about the science curriculum and its transaction in their respective schools.

As it was revealed earlier from the opinion of Headmasters that a class was divided into two sections if the number of students exceeded fifty. Usually there were two groups of science teachers, one for Physical Science and other for Natural Science. In the schools having no section needed two science teachers one each from the said groups. The number of teachers increased proportionately by the increase of sections. In actual practice particularly in BSE affiliated schools that science was taught even by the Arts teachers where the number of science teachers were not adequate. Many a times physical science teachers had to teach biological sciences and *vice-versa* in the absence of the other. However in CBSE affiliated sample schools such dislocation was not observed. As science is a practical-oriented subject laboratory assistant and attendants are required for better transactional work.

It was found that 16.66 percent CBSE sample schools did not have adequate science teaching staff while only 3.92 percent schools of BSE affiliated had laboratory attendants to conduct practicals. Most of the BSE schools were deprived of the services of the laboratory assistants. The number of periods allotted for science teaching per week was 32 in average while the same number of periods were also allotted for the teaching of other school subjects. Inadequacy of science teachers particularly in BSE affiliated schools were rampant. However, the condition was different and satisfactory in CBSE schools. These schools had adequate qualified teachers to transact the science curriculum.

It was revealed from the information provided by the science teachers that 37.82 percent teachers had more than 14 years of teaching experience to their credit while 60.86 percent had more than five years of experience and 1.32 percent teachers were having less than five years teaching experience. About 65.21 percent teachers have under gone in-service training course (Refresher and Orientation) and attended seminars organised from time to time to improve the teaching competencies of teachers. It was found that science teachers were able to feel that they could teach science effectively after being refreshed. However, 5.21 percent science teachers focussed on problems caused by overcrowded classes and lack of congenial transactional atmosphere. About 32.17 percent science teachers used to take extra classes to complete the course. Teachers who were lagging behind as compared to others with their own transitional work gave following reasons in support of their stand:

- Classes were over crowded.
- Students were not competent enough to understand the subject intellectually.
- Many teachers, particularly in private schools, did not get their salary in time, that too they were not paid adequately. But on record they receive full salary though in reality it was something different.
- Some were otherwise engaged as they were not satisfied with the place of their work.
- Students were not interested in studies.

As it was reported earlier by Headmasters that about 30 percent teachers undertook private tuition. It was felt by the teachers that there was a craze among parents to send their children for private tuition although the teachers took due care of the learners and to complete the course in time in the school itself. The reason in support of private tuition as revealed by the teachers were:

- Sufficient time was not available for effective transactional work in school.
- Individual attention could not be given regular classes.
- Home assignments could not be attended to in large size classes.
- Parents pressurised to take private tuition.
- Effective notes could not be given in regular classes which was time consuming process.

4.2.2 Science Room Facilities

It was quite evident from the information supplied by the sample school teachers that only 66.66 percent CBSE affiliated schools had separate science room/laboratory to conduct instructional work regularly. But about 96.07 percent BSE affiliated schools had no such facilities to conduct the classes. In those rooms or laboratories there were adequate facilities to conduct the classes. These classes have long wall black board, demonstration table, permanent demonstration of charts, facilities to exhibit some other charts as and when required, electric connections, permanent water supply, provision of gas cylinders to conduct experiments and well-equipped working tables fitted with water basins to be used by the students. But only 3.92 percent sample schools affiliated to BSE had such facilities. But in other schools regular transaction of science curricular activities were being conducted in regular class rooms alongwith other subjects. As a result of which science teaching became theoretical and monotonous. Very rarely some highly enthusiastic science teachers carry aids and support materials related to the topic to the class and demonstrated some experiments, etc. Otherwise the teachers mostly had to adopt lecturer method and rarely lecture-*cum*-discussion method of teaching. About 35.29 percent of BSE sample schools did not have even separate room to store science materials. The science materials were stored in some almirahs and kept in rooms alongwith other materials. In many schools even the science kit boxes remain unopened from the beginning itself and the reason stated by the teachers was lack of space in the school building to display the same.

The schools those had laboratory were mostly the CBSE affiliated schools. About 91.66 percent of them had most of the useful chemicals, useful equipment, safe burners and gas cylinders, fire extinguishers, basins, first aid kit, exhaust fans, etc., but in reality 25 percent of them were facing problems of shortage of fund to meet the demands of consumable items due to which they were not in a position to get sufficient amount of chemicals, apparatus and other consumable materials. No sample school had separate science book library but the science books were kept in general library alongwith other books. All most all the schools did not have sufficient books which could be kept in library to enhance or maintain scientific attitude or scientific temper of the students. Students were issued books to read as per their choice but never pursuaded to take books from library which could help to develop their scientific attitude and scientific temper. About 96.07 percent of BSE sample schools never subscribed regularly for any science magazine or journals to be used by the teachers and students. While 58.33 percent CBSE schools subscribed for science magazines. Teachers were of the opinion that the number of books, magazines and journals related to science was quite insufficient in their respective institutions.

4.2.3 Facilities of Teaching Aids

There are several aids to be used by the teachers to make the science education lively and comprehensive. About 66.54 percent of BSE affiliated sample schools did not have any scientific aids but they did have some charts related to different branches of science such as Botany, Zoology, Physics and Chemistry, etc. while 85 percent CBSE sample schools and rest of the BSE sample schools were in possession of more or less scientific aids, charts, kit box, maps, globes and boards of displaying scientific articles. Hardwares like Radio, Tape Recorder, Television, Film Projector, Slide Projector, Epidiascope, Microscope were not used in almost all BSE sample schools and in 36.64 percent of CBSE sample schools. It was clear from the above facts that the teachers were not getting appropriate teaching aids or support materials to facilitate transactional work effectively. It was also reported that about 35.21 percent teachers take aids prepared by themselves in their own interest. Those who were not using the audio-visual aids have given the following reasons:

- The aids were not available in 86.27 percent BSE and 25 percent CBSE schools.
- The aids were not sufficient as there were classes to be engaged simultaneously with those aids in 11.76 percent BSE and 8.30 percent CBSE schools.
- There was no scope for improvisation of such aids in 86.27 percent BSE and 41.66 percent CBSE schools.
- In the occasion of using audio-visual aids, it is difficult to complete the course in time.
- While using aids the students were getting diverted from the main points of discussion.
- There was no sufficient scope to use the aids even if those were available.

4.2.4 Other Facilities

It was revealed from the opinion of the sample teachers that except 41.66 percent CBSE schools there was no Botanical garden in any of the BSE and CBSE schools. Some schools have gardens but those were merely flowering garden for the beautification of the campus only. Those who had the garden opined that the gardens were poorly maintained. Students were neither asked to take part in gardening nor students were ever taken to garden intentionally for transactional work. Some times some specimens were collected from the garden for experimentation or demonstration in classes. Sometimes the specimens were used because of its availability. Barring a few CBSE schools no sample schools had science club. About 5 percent schools had science clubs but very much disorganised. No regular work was conducted in the club. It was just ornamental. No sample schools had Eco club. The reasons of not having functional clubs as mentioned by teachers were:

- No fund was available for such activities.
- No space was available in school premises for such activities.
- Neither the teachers nor the students were interested for such activities.
- Even if there were some enthusiastic teachers they were not permitted to collect funds from the students in that regards.
- If such activities were to be conducted lots of time was to be invested beyond school hour.
- Some teachers were of the opinion that those were unnecessary headache to the teachers' concerned.
- High achievers were not very much interested for such activities.

4.2.5 Co-curricular Activities

Science is a creative subject. It expands the horizon of intellectual queries. So co-curricular activities are very essential to ensure the involvement of students apart from particular study prescribed in courses of studies. These are supplementary activities to curricular activities. About 91.66 percent sample CBSE schools conducted activities like Field Trips, Project Work, Science Exhibition, Science Fair. Only 45.09 percent BSE sample schools organised such programmes. But rest of the sample schools in both the categories faced financial hurdles in organising such activities. In some schools problems like lack of interest among the teachers and students, sometimes authorities, etc. responsible for non-organisation of such activities. About 80.39 percent BSE sample schools and all CBSE sample schools participated in

Debate Competition, Essay Competition, Science Quiz conducted by different organisations. About 21.56 percent BSE and 66.66 percent CBSE sample schools participated in circle level science exhibition while 7.8 percent BSE and 58.33 percent CBSE schools participated at state level science exhibition programme. Organisation of inter-school competitions were also encouraged by educational authorities and it was found that about 78.43 percent BSE sample schools participated in such activities.

As the CBSE affiliated schools are not controlled by state educational authorities they had the problems of getting information of such activities being conducted at different levels, i.e. either at circle level, state level or national level as these activities were mostly conducted by district and state educational authorities. But all BSE schools used to get such information through their educational authorities. Firstly, sometimes the schools could not get information much before time as they required sufficient time for preparation. Secondly, even if they exhibit or students were selected for the purpose because of apathetic attitude of parents and some times educational authorities, teachers and students could not get scope for joining in such events. Thirdly, sometimes some teachers were so callous that they never persuade students to join in such activities. Fourthly, financial problems cause hindrances for students and teachers to participate in such activities.

However in average five such activities were conducted in sample schools for encouraging students to take part in co-curricular activities.

4.2.6 Assignments

Home assignments play a very positive role in all round development of the learner. A learner becomes capable of transferring his/her knowledge and understanding, gained through curricular transaction, to real life situation. Mostly the cognitive domains get enriched through different assignments. He/she develops the cognitive capacities such as logical reasoning, reflective thinking, problem-solving and using higher mental processes, develop attitude and feelings and psychomotor skills in life situations through different assignments.

4.2.7 Achievement of the Students in Scientific Activities

The effect of teaching can be assessed through many ways. A teacher feels very much satisfied when his/her product is assessed high by others. It brings satisfaction to both teachers and students. It was found that in average 37.25 percent students of BSE and 58.33 percent students of CBSE schools had owned awards at the school District, State, National Level in different competition held in science-related subjects. Those events were mostly science exhibition, debate competition, quiz and such other activities.

No BSE schools and 75 percent CBSE schools conducted monthly tests to ascertain students achievement in science. But all sample schools (both BSE and CBSE affiliated schools) conducted terminal examinations thrice in CBSE schools and twice in BSE schools. About 90 percent teachers of CBSE schools were of the opinion that the achievement of the students were good whereas the sample teachers of BSE schools were not satisfied with the performance of their students in science. But in average student responses were good in science class as opined by them.

4.2.8 Time-table

A scientifically prepared time-table acts as an catalytic agent to enhance better teaching-learning situation in the school. All the sample educational institutions took utmost care in preparing and practising effective time-table.

As revealed from the responses of science teachers in average 32 periods per week available per class in secondary stage. But to our surprise it was found that in BSE schools there was no scope for practical classes in school plant. All the classes were theoretical. A teacher usually demonstrate some experiments in theory classes. Students were mere spectators of these experiments demonstrated by the teachers. But in CBSE affiliated schools there was provision of practical classes in laboratory in their time-table. Students worked in the laboratory and received first hand experience under the supervision of teachers. Unlike BSE students the CBSE students enjoy more status and advantage as regards to the practical classes done in well furnished laboratory.

But the sample teachers of both the schools expressed their feelings to have more number of periods in science per week.

They felt difficulty in completing the course in specified time limit. Many times it seems they had to engage students in science teaching and learning by conducting some extra classes towards the end of session.

4.2.9 Course Content

There are many discussions resulting in revision of the courses prescribed in secondary school stage in general and science courses in particular. As many as 80 percent of BSE sample teachers felt that the content of science course was appropriate and befitting to the need of time, society and students. As it has been reported earlier that majority teachers could complete the courses in due time and in many cases science teachers also held to take extra classes for such purpose. Rest of the science teachers claimed the difficulty they come across because of the content difficulty and non-availability of teaching aids. The science course content had got enough of applied reflection of facts in real life situation.

Many teachers were of the opinion that the curricula prescribed by BSE and CBSE authorities though did not satisfy all the principle of curriculum construction still there were some what considerable effort of taking care of the principles of curriculum construction such as principles of utility, variety, need, relevance, readiness and flexibility. Still they recommended regular revision of the curricula to make it effective and update. Those, who found it difficult to complete the work during the session with the curriculum transaction posed different problems in support of their argument. Few of those stated problems were:

— Time duration 40 minutes for a period allotted for the science teaching was not sufficient.
— Number of periods allotted per week for science teaching were insufficient.
— Many topics have higher level of difficulty.
— Some of them were not able to take all the stipulated classes as they were otherwise busy in some other work of school.
— Overloaded syllabus.
— Because of extensive use of teaching aids as per requirement.

The opinion of sample teachers as regards the content matter have been presented in Table 4.2.1 on page 82.

TABLE 4.2.1
Opinion on Credibility of Content Matter in Science Syllabus

Items	*Percentage of frequency of positive response*		*Average percentage of frequency of positive response*	*Percentage of frequency of negative response*		*Average percentage of frequency of negative response*
	BSE	*CBSE*		*BSE*	*CBSE*	
Topics in a Class are enlargement of previous class	11.70	12.00	11.85	88.30	88.00	88.15
Presence of irrelevant content matter	16.66	20.00	18.33	83.34	80.00	81.67
Presence of many useful and important topics	83.33	80.00	81.66	16.67	20.00	18.33
Presence of content on applied aspect of science	72.70	78.00	75.35	27.30	22.00	24.65
Presence of upto-date information about modern development	78.80	78.00	78.40	21.20	22.00	21.60
Adequacy of content on applied aspect of science	72.22	69.80	71.01	27.78	30.20	28.99
Different branches of science proportionately represented	88.88	92.00	90.44	11.12	08.00	09.56
Existence of factual mistakes of the content matter	05.00	07.50	06.25	95.00	92.50	93.55

The Table 4.2.1 showed that topics in science syllabi were not merely enlargement of materials of previous classes. The syllabi contained least irrelevant content matter, useful and important topics, information about modern development in the field of science and technology, adequacy of the scope of application of knowledge in real-life situation and better representation of different branches of science. But it was a disgraceful fact that as many as 6.25 percent of teachers in average indicated about the presence of factual error in the discussion of content matter. Contents described in books prepared by BSE and CBSE suffered very much from the problem.

The sample teachers opined about the presence of different branches of science included in the syllabi which has been presented in Table 4.2.2.

TABLE 4.2.2
Different Branches of Science Reflected in Syllabi in Percentage

Branches of Science	*BSE Syllabus*	*CBSE Syllabus*	*Average*
Physics	35.00	40.00	37.50
Chemistry	30.00	25.00	27.50
Biology	20.00	25.00	22.50
Agriculture	07.00	05.00	06.00
Animal Husbandry	08.00	05.00	06.50

However, teachers expressed satisfaction as regards to the representation of different branches in the science syllabi.

4.2.10 Methods of Teaching

Methods of teaching plays pivotal role in making teaching-learning situation effective. Even teacher has got his/her own teaching style and at the same time each learner has his/her unique learning capability and technique. The teacher becomes acceptable because of his/her unique way of teaching. Which is an integral part of his/her unique personality. The teacher utilises teaching techniques his/her teaching which makes the subject interesting for the learners. Once learner develops interest with the teacher he starts liking to the subject. In reality no subject is dry or difficult which creates problem for the learners. The teacher makes the subject interesting for learners because of his/her acrobatics exhibited while interacting with the learners. Teacher is a social engineer who engineers in shaping the learning style with the learner which becomes an integral part of his personality. Because of this unique contribution of the teacher he/she is remembered by the learner for ever.

The responses of BSE affiliated school teachers revealed that usually they follow lecture, discussion, seldom demonstration-*cum*-discussion and observation methods while transacting science curriculum. But the CBSE teachers employed laboratory, project and assignment methods in addition to the methods followed by their counterparts in BSE schools. But it was found that most of the time the lecture method dominated the courses of interaction by the sample teachers irrespective of type of schools. The project and assignment methods were used in CBSE schools at times as it was a requirement of the course of interaction.

It was also found that majority sample schools did not subscribe for any journals in the field of methodology. Whatever information they gathered as regards to their improvement of ideas of methodology was through in-service training programmes and own experience. More than fifty percent teachers (52.22 percent of BSE and 60 percent of CBSE schools) revealed that they consulted/ discussed about the content matter whenever they feel its necessity. But this was not a regular feature among other sample teachers.

4.2.11 Text Book, Work Book and Reference Books

Though the students are very much dependent on text book, it is obvious but for teachers that it is just an aid. For the teachers journals and reference books along with text books are very essential for updating his knowledge. Text book, as a teacher feels, is an assets to control the process of teaching and evaluation. Hence, it becomes very difficult to ignore the contribution of text books, work books and reference books in the field of teaching and learning process.

It was revealed from the responses of CBSE teachers that the text books were made available to them very much in time where as it was a great problem particularly in rural BSE schools, some times even the urban BSE school students faced the problem as said by the sample teachers. Because of some organisational and administrative problems at BSE level text books could not be made ready for distribution.

As many as 18.33 percent in average of sample teachers of both the schools were not satisfied with the analysis and presentation of the content matter given in the text book. But 81.67 percent teachers average were quite satisfied with the present condition of text book. The following were the causes of dissatisfaction as listed from their responses: (1) Lots of ambiguities were there in the explanation of topic. (2) Authors were not very thorough about the content matters as a result of which the explanation some times lack conceptual clarity. (3) The illustrations and examples were not sufficient. (4) Some of the diagrams were not very much illustrative and some times factual mistakes prevailed there in. (5) The illustrations did not correlate some times with the problems arising out of real life situations.

There was no provision of work book in science in any type of schools. But 34.78 percent teachers of both the schools felt its necessity and they opined that special type work book should be made available up to Class X.

As many as 38.88 percent BSE teachers and 90 percent CBSE teachers were aware of journals related to science. The journals were as follows—Science Reporter, Junior Science Digest, Junior Science Refresher, Physics for You, Mathematics Today, Chemistry Today, Nature, Science Patron and Education Today.

Few teachers (64.34 percent) opined that, it was a necessity to go through the reference books but other teachers were silent about it. They felt that text book was sufficient enough for managing class room situation. They could not feel its necessity because of the following reasons: (1) These were not available in school library. (2) They could not feel to procure those on their own. (3) There was no other sources of procuring Journals and Magazine.

4.2.12 Some Specific Problems Faced by Science Teachers in Secondary School

When science teachers of the sample schools were encountered to reveal some specific problems they faced in the process of teaching-learning situation, they came out with sensual revelation about a different aspects of the problems they usually faced in school plant. Some of those are worth mentioning here.

4.2.12.1 Revelation of Facts as Regards to the Administrative Problem

Every secondary school was governed by a Headmaster/ Principal as its head. But in privately managed school the Headmasters/Principals were not able to enjoy enough freedom. There the managing committees which were quite active and they discharged most of the administrative functions in the school management. Headmaster became merely a rubber stamp.

The science teachers of the sample schools faced following administrative problems as indicated in the Table 4.2.3.

TABLE 4.2.3
Problems Related to Administration

Sl. No.	*Problem Items*	*Percentage of positive attitudinal frequency towards the problems*	*Percentage of negative attitudinal frequency towards the problems*	*Percentage of indifferent attitudinal frequency towards the problems*
1.	Inadequacy of time to prepare for Science classes because of professional preoccupation	34.78	57.39	07.83
2.	Non-availability of science text book	39.14	60.86	–
3.	Heavy workload	69.56	23.92	6.52
4.	Want of science hand as per the requirement of the school	71.74	21.73	6.53
5.	Promotion of the students to next higher class securing poor mark in science	17.84	81.73	0.43
6.	Absence of remedial teaching in time framework of the school	66.95	30.00	3.05
7.	Insufficiency of periods allotted in time framework of the school to cover syllabus	40.43	53.05	06.52
8.	Over crowded classes	65.20	30.00	4.80
9.	Irregularity in providing in-service training	71.73	23.06	5.21

Perusal of Table 4.2.3 indicated that majority sample teachers (53.05 percent) could not feel about the insufficiency of periods allotted in time framework to cover syllabus. But rest of the problems were quite prevalent in the schools which create hindrances in creation of congenial teaching-learning situation in the secondary classes.

4.2.12.2 Problems Related to Availability of In-service Training Programme

The present syllabi of secondary school science in CBSE and BSE schools have undergone many changes. It was felt that the teachers needed orientation training and refresher courses to update their knowledge in different fields of science and latest development in teaching techniques. It was also indicated by the Heads of the sample institutions that the in-service training programmes conducted for the science teachers were quite insufficient. The sample teachers were also carrying the same opinion. About 72.22 percent teachers of BSE schools and 70.00 percent of CBSE respondents opined that non-availability of in-service training programme created problem with their teaching. But few teachers (5.2 percent of both the schools) revealed their indifferent attitude towards this problems.

The teachers who expressed their difficulty in taking classes have suggested for extra training in the following areas of science which has been shown in Table 4.2.4.

TABLE 4.2.4
Requirements of Extra Training in Different Areas of Science Syllabus

Areas	*Frequency in percentage*
Waves	69.3
Magnetism and Electricity	48.5
Life Process	65.6
Solar Energy	67.2
Nuclear Energy	79.4
Fossil Fuel	44.7

Many teachers (56.66 percent from BSE and 30 percent from CBSE sample schools) did not aware of the process of taking chances of in-service training programmes. Organisations like NCERT, SCERT, BSE, CBSE who organises in-service programmes were mostly dependent on the educational administrative authorities of the state to sponsor the names of the science teachers for undergoing training in such programmes. The teachers provided following reasons of not able to avail the chances of such programmes:

- Selection procedure adopted by the educational authorities was unsystematic.

- Institutions randomly selected teachers without having any logic.
- Partiality was a regular feature, many times due to which few teachers chances frequently and others were deprived of.
- Information for attending courses usually not received in time. Many times it reaches to the teacher after the expiry of the programme.
- Even they get the chances, many times the Heads of institutions do not relieve them with the plea of exigencies of services.
- The information about programmes do not reach to concerned institution.
- The following are the suggestion provided by the teachers for availing chances in in-service programmes.
- The information about in-service-programmes should be notified to the schools through the authorities sufficiently ahead of its commencement.
- Options should be taken by the educational authorities as well as schools quite in advance of commencement of the programme.
- No one should be given frequent chances to attend such programmes.
- Duration of the programme should be minimum of 5 days and maximum of 15 days.
- Programmes should be conducted during vacation.
- Call for the programme to attend should reach to participant and concerned authorities quite in advance.

4.2.12.3 Problems Related to Curriculum Transaction

It was found from the responses of sample teachers dealing with science curriculum transaction that they were not very much satisfied with it. They encountered many problems related to curriculum and its transaction. Their views have been presented in Table 4.2.5 on page 89.

By and large it was revealed from the opinion of the sample teachers that there was problem inherent in curriculum transaction in both BSE and CBSE schools. Teachers were facing almost similar type of difficulties as the two curricula of both the boards were

TABLE 4.2.5

Problems Related to Curricular Transaction

Sl. No.	*Problem Items*	*Positive response in percentage*	*Negative response in percentage*	*Indifference response in percentage*
1.	Syllabus in science is quite heavy	31.74	68.26	–
2.	Objective of teaching science are achievable through present curriculum	62.60	35.65	1.75
3.	Contents of syllabus are away from real life situation	8.69	90.0	1.31
4.	Science syllabus is not comprehensive	23.91	74.34	1.75
5.	There are difficulties in transacting some activities due to content difficulty	41.30	58.70	–
6.	There is less link between content matters of two successive classes	15.21	79.58	5.21
7.	The content matters have not been arranged se-quetially and logically	9.13	89.56	1.30

more or less same. The CBSE curricula was having a bit supremacy over the BSE because of inclusion of practical work and higher scientific theory in secondary stage. The BSE schools had little scope for practical work while transacting the science curriculum. But it was a common opinion that topics on magnetism, generation of electricity, organisation of living world, nuclear energy, solar energy and the universe required to be more sequential and logical. Even some teachers (8.69 percent) suggested that it was difficult to relate few topics like Nuclear reactor, Space exploration, Cell division, etc. with the experience of learners in real life situation. About 24.34 percent suggested for more elaboration of some topics included in the syllabi.

Although the teachers were not facing serious problems to teach the content matter but few (45.65 percent) expressed views that they faced difficulties in transacting some topics like chemical bonding and reaction, magnetism and electricity organisation of living world, solar energy and nuclear energy.

4.2.12.4 Problems Related to Laboratory Facilities

As reported by almost all (96.07 percent) BSE schools and very few (33.34 percent) CBSE schools did not have proper laboratory facilities, for which the science teachers faced some specific difficulties in transaction curricular activities. Even 28.99 percent teachers opined that there was no applied aspects of science as per the contents included in the syllabus. It is also noted that in science room 87.82 percent teachers found the problems arising due to lack of demonstration table and other working facilities. About 47.39 percent teachers faced problems in teaching because of non-availability of charts and other graphics. While 63.04 percent teachers faced the problems of other facilities like water supply, gas supply, etc. The sample teachers of BSE and CBSE schools have suggested the following few but very essential aids which could be of much importance while transacting science curricular activities in addition to regular materials already in their possession.

Equipment

Formulation of Chemical Bond, Wave Motion apparatus, Ohm's Law Verification apparatus, Dry Cell, Electrical Cell, Rheostat, Motor Dynamo, Telescope, Compound Microscope, Manometer, Solar Cooker, Solar Cell, Turbine (working model), etc.

Charts

Charts on discovery of electron, proton and neutron and chemical bonding of different molecules, Mendalives periodic table, charts on cell division, different parts of plant, human physiology kidney, blood circulation, skin, cell structure and structure of cell organelles tissue and tissue system of plants and animals, nuclear fission, different types of food, bio-geo-chemical (gaseous, sedimentary) cycles, diseases caused due to food to food deficiency, ecological balance, extraction of metals and pyramid of food chain and web, etc.

Models

Human skulls, human skeleton, skull bone of different types of man in different geological periods, human heart, kidney, human eye and ear, wind mill, solar cell, solar system and biogas plant.

The laboratory deficient schools opined that the sample schools were suffering from following problems:

- Schools were not provided with water, gas and electricity supply.
- There was no specific well equipped store rooms for keeping the apparatus and chemicals safely.
- Lack of student gallery in the school.
- Absence of science attendants and laboratory assistants.
- Non-availability of specious class rooms.
- Poor-ventilation system/design in class room.
- Non-availability of botanical garden and acquarium.
- Non-availability of time for displaying the apparatus before the class.

It was clear from these findings that teacher could provide theoretical knowledge. There was not much co-ordination of theoretical knowledge with the practical skill. The conceptual clarity of students could not be brought to the level of the satisfaction. The psychomotor and effective domain of learners became dormant due to which cognition could not be full-fledged.

4.2.12.5 Problems Related to Instructional Materials

Library is one of the most essential branch of the school. There should be provision of different types of science-related books in the library. Those must be prescribed text-books, supplementary inspirational science books, background books, reference books, popular science-related books, few standard magazine and journals.

After encountering with the sample teachers it was found that 85.71 percent schools in average faced the problems of non-availability of magazine and journals in different aspects of science and technology. The other information as regards to the problems can be very well studied from the Table 4.2.6.

Perusal of Table 4.2.6 showed that 62.22 percent teachers in average were facing problems as regards the non-availability of teachers' guide or hand books. It was suggested that they require magazine and journals like Science Reporter, Aloka, Vijnanaloka, Physics for You, Chemistry Today, Mathematics Today, Readers' Digest, Wisdom, Education Today, Junior Science Digest, etc.

TABLE 4.2.6
Problems Related to Instructional Materials Available in Schools

Problem Items	*Percentage of frequency of teachers facing the problems*			*Percentage of frequency of teachers not facing the problems*			*Percentage of frequency possessing indifferent attitude*		
	BSE	*CBSE*	*Ave.*	*BSE*	*CBSE*	*Ave.*	*BSE*	*CBSE*	*Ave.*
1. Non availability of magazine, journals in Science subjects	94.44	76.00	85.22	5.56	24.00	14.78	—	—	—
2. Non-availability of reference books related to course	87.25	38.00	62.62	12.75	62.00	38.37	—	—	—
3. Non-availability of teachers' guide and Hand books	94.44	30.00	62.22	5.56	70.00	37.78	—	—	—
4. Mechanical getup and printing of the books	10.55	10.00	10.27	82.79	86.70	84.39	6.66	4.00	5.73
5. Organisation of subjects matter in the prescribed text book	13.88	4.00	8.94	44.54	94.00	69.27	8.58	2.00	5.29

4.2.12.6 Problems Related to Classroom Situation

The findings in this area is given in Table 4.2.7.

The perusal of Table 4.2.7 indicated that some of the problems were quite serious as opined by the teachers. Those problems were, students fail to understand new topics, because they forget the previous lessons, students used to come to class without completing home task, difficult to engage students in practical classes, difficult to improve teaching aids in the classroom and difficulty to tackle individual difference in regular class room situation.

4.2.12.7 Problems Related to Methodology of Teaching

It was found from the collected data that sample teachers from both CBSE and BSE schools opined with similar views and they expressed that it was difficult to follow demonstration method by 90 percent, lecturer-*cum*-demonstration method by 66.95 percent, problems solving method by 82.17 percent, project method by 93.91 percent, laboratory method by 92.17 percent, due to the

TABLE 4.2.7
Problems Related to Classroom Situation

Problem Items	*Percentage of Positive frequency of teachers*			*Percentage of negative frequency of teachers*			*Percentage of indifferent frequency of teachers*		
	BSE	*CBSE*	*Ave.*	*BSE*	*CBSE*	*Ave.*	*BSE*	*CBSE*	*Ave.*
1. Difficult to meet the queries of students in the classroom	16.66	4.00	10.33	73.34	94.00	83.67	10.00	2.00	6.00
2. Hesitation of students to attend science class regularly	6.11	0.00	3.05	93.80	100.00	96.94	0.00	0.00	0.00
3. Students are unmindful in the class room	14.44	6.00	10.22	77.78	90.00	83.89	7.77	4.00	5.80
4. Students, interaction with the teacher in the classroom	73.33	94.00	83.66	20.56	2.00	11.28	6.11	4.00	5.05
5. Students fail to understand new topics as they forget the previously taught topics	58.33	8.00	33.16	33.90	84.00	58.95	7.77	6.00	6.80
6. Students come to class without completing home work	25.00	2.00	13.50	67.78	94.00	80.89	7.22	4.00	5.61
7. Difficult to do practical in science	13.88	2.00	7.94	77.79	96.00	86.89	8.33	2.00	5.16
8. Difficult to improve teaching aids in the classroom	13.33	10.00	11.66	80.03	86.00	83.96	6.66	4.00	5.33
9. Difficult to help each student individually in the class	94.44	96.00	95.22	5.56	4.00	4.78	0.00	0.00	0.00

inherent difficulties present with a particular method. As many as 7.1 percent teachers used to utilise a method which was the combination of different strategies of teaching and it was of their own. They could develop their own teaching style to meet the exigencies. But majority (52.17 percent) teachers failed in this respect. They could not able to overcome the problems arising out of the specific methodology of teaching in classroom situation. As opined by 66.95 percent teachers that it was difficult to pursue the methods of teaching properly as syllabus was heavy, lack of teaching materials in 69.59 percent cases and lack of proper facilities for developing different strategies like laboratory and project methods, etc. Besides there were 76.95 percent teachers felt that there was no provision for utilising the scope for the students learning science outside the school.

4.2.12.8 Problems Related to Organising Co-curricular Activities

As co-curricular activities are supplementary activities to curricular aspect its importance cannot be ignored in teaching and learning process. But unfortunately it was found that 80.00 percent sample teachers expressed their difficulty in organising different co-curricular activities in school plant. Even 56.52 percent teachers opined that they faced difficulty in relating science contents with real life situations due to want of co-curricular activities. The hindrances in organising such activities was mainly due to non-availability of resources. Very few sample teachers (5.21 percent) stated that they felt it difficult to relate science with other subjects in course of teaching. The reasons of organising such activities stated by them were lack of funds, lack of proper interest among teachers, lack of time and space and lack of proper facilities in school plant, etc. Some examples of difficulties felt by majority of sample teachers in organising different co-curricular activities are worth mentioning here.

Activities	***Difficulties***
Science Exhibition	Lack of laboratory facilities, funds, space and materials.
Field Trips	Lack of time, funds, interest and co-operation from concerned corners.
Science Museum	Lack of space, funds and interest.
Debates and Eloquation	No provision of extra time in school routine lack of interest and co-operation of authority and teachers as well. Other activities like exhibiting documentary film shows observance of birth day of great scientists, science club activities, observation of environment day, etc. were not organised mainly due to lack of funds in schools, interest among teachers and co-operation of authorities.

4.2.12.9 Problems Related to Evaluation

Evaluation is a process of appraising the nature of evidence about the achievements of pupils in a particular subject. Its main aim is to improve the quality of education process and individual as a whole. It measures the performances of a pupil in scholastic and non-scholastic areas. The opinion of the teachers have been tabulated in Table 4.2.8.

TABLE 4.2.8
Problems Related to Evaluation

Problem Items	*Percentage of frequency of teachers facing the problems*			*Percentage of frequency of teachers not facing the problems*			*Percentage of frequency of teachers having indifferent attitude*		
	BSE	*CBSE*	*Ave.*	*BSE*	*CBSE*	*Ave.*	*BSE*	*CBSE*	*Ave.*
1. Difficulty in assessing the progress of students regularly	37.77	10.00	23.88	50.86	88.00	69.43	11.36	02.00	06.68
2. Non-availability of readymade diagnostic tests to identify learning difficulty of students in science	81.66	60.00	70.83	09.33	34.00	21.66	09.00	06.00	07.50
3. Difficulty in correcting home assignments of students in science	61.11	24.00	42.55	38.88	76.00	57.44	0.00	0.00	0.00
4. Difficult to evaluate the non-scholastic competence of the learners	97.97	60.00	78.85	02.03	40.00	21.51	0.00	0.00	0.00
5. Difficult to prepare test items for a test in science	06.66	00.00	03.33	85.57	98.00	91.78	07.77	02.00	09.88

An analysis of the Table 4.2.8 indicated that 78.85 percent tachers in average could find difficulty in assessing by the non-scholastic competence of the students. They were interested to procure a standardised diagnostic test to identify learning difficulties rather than preparing one by their own. As many as 91.78 percent teachers in average pointed out that they could not face any difficulty in preparing test items. It was found that the process of evaluation posed a challenging task in front of the working teachers.

The teachers of both BSE and CBSE schools posed some of the common problems which they come across. Firstly, some teachers provide private tuition to overcome financial problems they face. Secondly, the shortage of teaching hands in handling physical science and natural science classes creates problems in science teaching. Thirdly, frequent transfer of the teachers dislocates course completion and planned learning activities. Fourthly, many times a single science teacher is to transact the whole science courses of different classes in a school, which cause unusual work load and strain.

The Chi-square (χ^2) values were calculated for all the items provided in the questionnaire related to different areas of the problems. The items which posed as problems by the teachers and the items which are not considered as the problems were identified. The items and their level of significance are shown in Tables 4.2.9 and 4.2.10.

TABLE 4.2.9
Significance of Chi-square (χ^2) Values for Responses which are Posed by Majority Teachers as Problems

Sl. No.	*Responses posed as problems by the sample teachers*	*Value of of χ^2*	*Level of Significance*
1.	Time is inadequate to plan for science teaching	5.14	0.05
2.	Non-availability of science teachers as per requirement of schools	21.72	0.01
3.	Students are promoted to next higher class securing poor marks in science	31.58	0.01
4.	No provision of remedial teaching in science in time table	9.18	0.01
5.	Overcrowd classes	8.58	0.01
6.	Syllabus in science teaching is heavy	9.78	0.01
7.	All objectives of teaching are not achievable	4.13	0.05
8.	There is no science laboratory in the school	60.35	0.01
9.	No provision of science equipment	6.30	0.01
10.	School does not have working laboratory benches	42.26	0.01
11.	School does not have demonstration table for conducting experiment	49.72	0.01
12.	School does not have necessary chart as per syllabus	8.92	0.01

(Contd.)

TABLE 4.2.9 (*Contd.*)

Sl. No.	*Responses posed as problems by the sample teachers*	*Value of χ^2*	*Level of Significance*
13.	School doe not have necessary models as per syllabus	4.12	0.05
14.	The journals and magazines in science are not available in school library	33.81	0.01
15.	Reference books are not available	5.30	0.05
16.	Teacher's guide/Handbooks are not available	21.24	0.01
17.	Students forget previously taught topics and fail to understand new topics	17.50	0.01
18.	Students attend class without completing home assignment	26.40	0.01
19.	Difficult to conduct practical classes in science	31.55	0.01
20.	Difficult to improvise teaching aids in science in the class room	15.55	0.01
21.	Difficult to help each student in the class	60.34	0.01
22.	(a) Problems to follow demonstration method	43.21	0.01
	(b) Demonstration-*cum*-Discussion method	7.55	0.01
	(c) Problem-solving method	31.55	0.01
	(d) Laboratory method	53.15	0.01
	(e) Project method	64.12	0.01
23.	Difficult to follow proper method to teaching due to:		
	(a) Inadequacy of time to manage heavy syllabus	17.50	0.01
	(b) Lack of materials	13.72	0.01
	(c) Lack of facilities for project and laboratory method	53.15	0.01
24.	No effort for utilising scope for students outside school for learning science	26.32	0.01
25.	Difficult to organise co-curricular activities in science	24.01	0.01
26.	Difficult to assess the progress of students in science regularly	7.55	0.01
27.	Difficult to evaluate the non-scholastic competency of learners	31.55	0.01

TABLE 4.2.10

Significance of χ^2 Values for Responses which are not Posed by Majority Teachers as Problems

Sl. No.	*Responses posed as non-problems by the sample teachers*	*Value of χ^2*	*Level of Significance*
1.	Content envisaged in syllabus are away from real life situation	45.4	0.01
2.	Comprehensiveness of syllabus	16.74	0.01

(Contd.)

Table 4.2.10 (*Contd.*)

Sl. No.	*Responses posed as non-problems by the sample teachers*	*Value of* χ^2	*Level of Significance*
3.	There is less link in between the content matters of two successive classes	26.26	0.01
4.	Topics in text books have not been arranged sequentially and logically	40.12	0.01
5.	Mechanical getup and printing of science text book	43.20	0.01
6.	Presentation and organisation of subject matter	40.20	0.01
7.	Students hesitated to attend science classes regularly	38.25	0.01
8.	Students remain unmindful in the science class	12.06	0.01
9.	Students hesitate to take interest with teachers in science class	8.34	0.01
10.	Teaching methods followed by the teacher:		
	(a) Text-book method	49.72	0.01
	(b) Lecture method	40.12	0.01
	(c) Discussion method	31.55	0.01
	(d) Combination of some methods	49.72	0.01
11.	Difficult to relate science with other subjects	5.15	0.05
12.	Difficult to prepare test items for a test in science	40.12	0.01

The perusal of Table 4.2.9 indicated that there is existence of problems faced by the teachers. Those problems required immediate attention to bring conducive situation in teaching-learning condition. The items specified in Table 4.2.10 were not real problems. If at all some were of the opinion that those problems might be due to lack of involvement on the part of teachers. The teachers are to be made responsible to deal with those problems effectively so as to make classroom situation conducive to enhance learning ability of learners.

4.3 INFORMATION AVAILABLE FROM THE STUDENTS OF BSE AND CBSE AFFILIATED SAMPLE SCHOOLS

4.3.1 General Information

Information from the students of BSE and CBSE affiliated sample schools were collected through a questionnaire developed in this regard. As regards the Geo-physical conditions of school it was found that the BSE affiliated schools were spread all over the state while CBSE affiliated schools were concentrate mostly in urban areas. Altogether opinions of 400 (Four hundred) BSE school students and 100 (One hundred) CBSE school students as regards the science teaching-learning conditions were collected.

As science teaching condition of schools is the main focus of the study it was revealed that numerical strength of teachers were almost adequate as per the requirements of school. The school having no additional sections have two science teachers, one to teach PCM (Physics, Chemistry and Mathematics) while another to teach CBZ (Chemistry, Botany and Zoology).

The following facts reveal the feelings of the students towards staff related to science teaching, science room facilities, aids and other facilities available in schools, more so about the co-curricular activities, assignments given by the teachers, time-table, course content, text book, conditions of both CBSE and BSE schools in Orissa. The information collected from the students were quantified section-wise as mentioned. The 'Yes' responses were given weightage of 2 (two) whereas 'No' responses were given weightage of 1 (one) only. The section-wise Mean and SD related to both the type of schools were calculated and the significance of difference have been estimated through 't' test.

4.3.2 Feeling of Students Towards Science Teaching Personnel

The response received from the students related to the position and effectiveness of science teaching personnel have been tabulated in Table 4.3.1.

TABLE 4.3.1

Difference between the BSE and CBSE Sample Schools in Staff Related to Science Teaching

Sl.No.	*Types of Schools*	*Mean*	*SD*	*'t'*	*Level of Significance*
1.	CBSE	38.65	3.61	14.28	0.01
2.	BSE	34.25	2.50		

The perusal of Table 4.3.1 indicated that the situation in these two type of schools differed significantly. The BSE schools were under staffed. There were neither science laboratory nor laboratory assistants in any schools. Only few schools did have laboratory attendants. But some of the CBSE schools did have laboratory attendants and other facilities as informed by the students. Some specific schools like Demonstration Multipurpose School, Bhubaneswar which is attached to Regional Institute of Education (RIE),

Bhubaneswar and is a constituent of NCERT had laboratory assistants. Other schools did not have such facilities. They manage their work mostly by the teachers who were assisted by the attendants whenever called upon.

As the students opined they were quite dependent on teachers as the difficulty level of science as a subject was higher as compared to other subjects like social studies and language. This section of the questionnaire mostly dealt with the interpersonal relationship in between teachers and taught which occupies a greater importance in relation to teaching and learning conditions prevailed in the schools. The following areas in relation to students' feeling have been taken into considerations while analysing interpersonal relationship. Those are cordiality of teachers towards the students, regularity of teachers in taking classes, effective completion of courses in the classes, sympathetic attitude of teachers towards students, relationship of students and teachers at personal level, field visit, responsibility of teachers for the weak students in remedial classes, effective teaching in a social atmosphere, impartiality of teachers towards students in the process of evaluation, demonstration of scientific experiments, accountability and academic excellence of teachers and some other information provided about the teachers.

4.3.3 Science Room Facilities

The dissimilarities of science room facilities between BSE and CBSE affiliated schools is indicated in Table 4.3.2.

TABLE 4.3.2
Dissimilarities between CBSE and BSE Sample Schools as Regards Science Room Facilities

Sl.No.	*Types of Schools*	*Mean of the science room facilities*	*SD*	*'t'*	*Level of Significance*
1.	CBSE	34.45	2.42	32.90	0.01
2.	BSE	23.10	3.23		

The perusal of Table 4.3.2 indicated that the two categories of schools differed significantly at 0.01 level as regards the science room facilities in the school premises. The BSE school science room facilities presented a dismal figure. There were many schools having no gallery type room for science teaching. Black boards were fitted on wall and no BSE schools and many CBSE schools had movable black boards. It was also seen that many BSE sample schools did not have demonstration table. There were facilities to exhibit the maps, charts on the wall at the time of need because there was no specific earmarked room for science teaching. The schools were electrified but most of the BSE schools had no water supply facility. But CBSE schools were electrified and had water supply facilities. The CBSE schools had demonstration tables and basins fitted with it, many CBSE schools were capable of procuring LPG Gas for use at the time of experimental need.

However, there was no special science library in any school of both CBSE and BSE categories but these schools kept science books alongwith other books in general library. In many schools the number of books were not sufficient to meet the requirement of students.

The necessary chemicals, equipments, gas lamp, gas cylinder, fire extinguisher, exhaust fan and First aid box were available in most of the CBSE schools while many BSE schools suffered from insufficiency of these items and some schools had lack of many such facilities. Regarding the chemicals and other consumable items BSE schools suffered from insufficiency and some CBSE schools faced the inadequacy of such materials.

Laboratory and its condition was not upto satisfaction in many schools of both CBSE and BSE categories although its importance for Science Education could not be underestimated rather most of the BSE schools showed specific absence of laboratory.

4.3.4 Teaching Aids or Support Material Facilities

The Mean difference between the two categories of schools as regards the availability of teaching aids or support materials have been presented in Table 4.3.3.

TABLE 4.3.3

Difference between the two Categories of Sample Schools as Regards the Availability of Teaching Aids

Sl.No.	*Types of Schools*	*Mean*	*SD*	*'t'*	*Level of Significance*
1.	CBSE	33.65	2.55	44.28	0.01
2.	BSE	22.35	2.21		

The perusal of Table 4.3.3 indicated that the difference between CBSE and BSE affiliated schools as regards availability of teaching aids or support materials differed significantly at 0.01 level. The facilities of teaching aids and support materials have got immense importance in teaching-learning process of science. Even without it the process is incomplete.

Charts, diagrams, other graphic aids and all other related materials in teaching science subjects like Botany, Zoology, Physics and Chemistry were available to some extent in all the sample schools of BSE and CBSE affiliated categories. However numbers of such materials very significantly between the two categories of schools. The CBSE schools had large varieties of aids or support materials. The BSE schools had lot of limitations because of one or other reasons.

Science kitbox is an essential equipment which bears high importance for teaching science. Some of the CBSE schools did have kit boxes while the BSE schools lacked it. As per the tabulated values the difference between two categories of schools was significant. Other required machineries such as globe, maps, boards for displaying scientific articles were available to some extent in all the schools. Audio-visual aids such as Radio, Tape Recorder, Record Players, Television, Film Projector and Slide Projector, Epidiascope, Microscope, etc. were available in some CBSE schools only.

4.3.5 Other Facilities

Other facilities like botanical garden, herbarium, acquarium, science club, museum, eco club, etc. are also play an important role in learning science. These help a lot to teacher to make his endeavour a success. The availability of such facilities have been indicated in Table 4.3.4.

TABLE 4.3.4
Difference between other Related Facilities Available in Two Categories of Sample Schools

Sl. No.	*Types of Schools*	*Mean*	*SD*	*'t'*	*Level of Significance*
1.	CBSE	14.35	2.24	8.65	0.01
2.	BSE	12.25	1.86		

A close look to the Table 4.3.4 revealed that there was significant difference between the BSE and CBSE affiliated sample schools as regard to the facilities like Botanical Garden, Science Clubs, etc. Botanical Garden, Herbarium, Aquarium, etc. provide living experience to students and ensure experiments effective in science teaching. It was found that more or less every schools had its own garden but few schools of the CBSE category used it as per the requirements of science teaching. It was also found that several schools used the garden for seasonal production of vegetables and fruits. Some schools used these gardens for growing flowers for decoration but for the specific purpose of science teaching usually they had not grown the garden.

Science club became a distant dream to many schools. There was no BSE sample school having science club but few CBSE schools had science laboratory which they said as club where scientific chart, diagrams specimens, machineries and aids were found for use of students and teachers.

4.3.6 Co-curricular Activities

The co-curricular activities are supplementary in nature to curricular activities in science teaching. These activities provide insight both to learners and teachers for better understanding of their responsibilities. As it seems more or less in every school these activities were conducted. The comparative situation as regards has been present in Table 4.3.5.

TABLE 4.3.5
Differences in Conducting Co-curricular Activities in both Categories of Sample Schools

Sl. No.	*Types of Schools*	*Mean*	*SD*	*'t'*	*Level of Significance*
1.	CBSE	16.60	2.81	8.76	0.01
2.	BSE	13.80	2.03		

A look to Table 4.3.5 indicated that the difference between the CBSE and BSE affiliated sample schools in conducting co-curricular activities was significant at 0.01 level. It was found that allmost all the schools organised co-curricular activities related to science teaching. Few CBSE schools organised study tour, field study and project work while no sample BSE schools conducted such activities, but many of them participated in science exhibition conducted by different agencies and hold picnics to different spots of environmental importance. The CBSE schools organised science exhibition in their school premises alongwith participation in science exhibition at District, State and National levels also.

Other activities like debate competition, essay competition, eloquence competition and science quiz were practised by the CBSE schools but it took place in some of the BSE schools only.

4.3.7 Assignments Provided to the Students

Assignment and home tasks are integral part of the formal education process. It plays specific catalytic role to extend the impact of schools upto the homes of the students. Only 20 percent of BSE and 68 percent students of CBSE affiliated sample school students respectively opined that home tasks were carefully verified by the school teachers. Almost no BSE school conduct monthly science test but even if it was conducted by a few these tests were not seriously taken. Follow-up actions were not geared in any case to rectify the defects and problems detected by the use of these tests while 37 percent students opined that teachers checked thoroughly the assignments submitted by them and used to give necessary remarks for corrections in respect of the CBSE schools. About 70 percent CBSE schools organised monthly tests on science and sent marks to the parents for necessary action at their end. Hence, it may be inferred from the above analysis that CBSE schools stand ahead in conducting assignment programmes to the BSE schools.

4.3.8 Time-table

Time-table is an imperative aspect for smooth functioning of institutions where the teachers are to take utmost care for the implementation of science course. There is provision of experimentation and practical work in time-table which is taken up carefully in CBSE schools. There are about three theory (one each for physics, chemistry and biology) and six practical classes (two each for physics, chemistry and biology) for science teaching in the CBSE schools and the students were taken to laboratory in these periods for experiment-*cum*-theory classes. However, some teachers used to take few extra practical classes beyond the schedule if required.

However, in the BSE schools students got eight science theory classes per week. There were no special periods for science practical but some enthusiastic teachers used to arrange few practical works/experiments in theory classes. They demonstrated some activities as opined by the students in course of teaching in theory classes. In both the types of schools the science classes were placed in time-table in a scattered way. No specific procedure seems to be followed in allocating the science classes during a weeks time.

4.3.9 Course Content/Text Book

It has got utmost importance for learners. Mostly the learners are dependent on text books for learning science. The opinion of students about the effect of text book in respect of both type of schools has been shown in Table 4.3.6.

TABLE 4.3.6
Difference of Opinion of Learners of Sample Schools on Text book

Sl. No.	*Types of Schools*	*Mean*	*SD*	*'t'*	*Level of Significance*
1.	CBSE	15.10	3.20	0.43	ns.
2.	BSE	15.25	2.94		

Many students of both types of schools expressed their satisfaction with the existing course content for the different classes of Secondary Education. There were few science books which were available in school library as opined by learners. The BSE school students were not at all satisfied with the pictorial presentation while the CBSE students felt better. Students of both the category sample schools had to say a little about the text book and almost they expressed their satisfaction as regards it.

It was opined that contents of science text books were well selected but they were not able to completely dependent on it. The sample students had to be dependent on some outside books for better learning to substantiate the deficiency they found from the text book. Text book was not sufficient for learning the entire contents of the syllabus. It was observed that sometimes students used to take the help of guide and key books or so called refresher books for their study.

From the above discussion and the Table 4.3.6 it is clear that the difference between the CBSE and the BSE affiliated schools as regards course content and text book is not significant in many respect rather there is similarity between the two categories in certain specific area.

4.4 OPINION OF SCIENCE SUPERVISORS AND EXPERTS

The opinion of science supervisors and experts were sought to assess the overall condition of science teaching-learning situations in classroom curricular structure, and methodology of teaching and different aspects of science education. The Science Supervisors and Experts were also requested to point out the problems of science teaching and suggest measures for its improvement. Thus their opinions have been summarised as mentioned below:

4.4.1 Course Content of Science

The syllabus and the contents incorporated there in occupy an important position in the teaching-learning process. Science as a subject has definite content to be a taught at different stages of education in different ways. The objectives and content of science as a subject is undergoing rapid changes in the present-age keeping learning with development of new knowledge and social change. The placement of content matter including the objectives of science subject needs to be flexible and dynamic to adhere the changes occurred around the world.

However, 80 percent of the respondents have expressed their satisfaction over the science curriculum and its appropriateness to the present time while 20 percent respondents have visualised the problems of science education, syllabus and content as given below:

- Overcrowded with clumsy facts and figures.
- Printing errors in Text-books.
- Ambiguous presentation of facts.
- Lack of adequate illustration and explanation.
- Lack of graphical representation.

However, significant difference was felt between the CBSE and the BSE courses. The CBSE text book contained elaborate and illustrated contents with adequate examples while the BSE courses suffered from several deficiencies as felt by the Experts. Those were:

- Lack of sufficient illustrations.
- Irrelevant presentation of fact.

But a few Experts were of the opinion that the CBSE text books were not up to mark because students as beginners felt very difficult to go through the books. They were mostly dependents on refreshers or some other books which were written by private agencies. The text books content presentation were full of clumsy facts and figures. Rather, the books were helpful for those who aspired for appearing at different competitive examinations.

In the BSE affiliated schools, as it was revealed earlier about the absence of laboratory in many schools. Because the students were not exposed to laboratory there was need of more elaboration of facts with examples. The effort in this regard was felt by some experts to be incorporated specifically in the text book. But whatever existing at the moment were not sufficient and were far away from satisfaction.

Further the distribution of content areas has got subject orientation, i.e. Physics, Chemistry, Biology both in the BSE and CBSE curriculum. As it revealed that 75 percent Science Experts and Supervisors expressed their satisfaction over the content distribution. While 25 percent of them reported their dissatisfaction about subjectwise in both the curricula. They were of the opinion that there should be proper integration between the subject instead of specific subject-based orientations. It should be presented in the form of General Science rather than individual subject form. The subject orientations could be started from +2 level.

4.4.2 Methods of Teaching

Method of teaching plays a pivotal role in the process of education in general and in science teaching in particular. It is a communication process between the teacher and taught. It has got subject and grade-wise orientations and even topic-wise orientations. It was revealed from the respondents that in 70.58 percent BSE schools and 53 percent CBSE schools science subject was taught in traditional and most unpsychological text-book reading method. There were several causes of such irregularity and some of those as expressed were lack of laboratory facilities.

Lack of teaching aids or support materials to teach the topic and lack of enthusiastic teachers, uncongenial school and class room climate, etc. Use of teaching aids to teach science is imperative because scientific theories carries practical aspects. Rather the need of proper demonstration and experimentation are most essential. Method of teaching must be accomplished with teaching aids for a congenial atmosphere of teaching-learning situation. There are different kinds of hardwares starting from chalk board to most sophisticated computer, television, tape recorder and radio, etc. These have massive use in the class room situation to ensure better learning of students. The development in the field of science and technology has directed impact on the class room. The transaction of the contents of science must be based on hierarchical cognitive development. Teaching aids not only encourages students for better way of learning but also provides relaxation to a teacher in his class room. About 89 percent science experts have expressed their concern over the poor use of teaching aids as regards time and context both. It was also revealed that there were schools where the concerned authorities were least bothered to provide such facilities. The difference as regards such facilities between the BSE and the CBSE schools was quite significant. The Science Supervisors and Experts felt the necessity of improving laboratory conditions in the schools. They emphasised on the appointment of laboratory assistants and attendants, creation of Botanical garden in the schools and budgetary provision for financing the schools for the said purpose.

4.4.3 Co-curricular Activities

Co-curricular activities should be supplemented with co-curricular activities to make teaching-learning process purposeful, effective and interesting. The provision of co-curricular activities in the BSE schools was inadequate as they felt. There were also several schools, who were not interested to organise or participate in such activities due to lack of funds and lack of enthusiasm on the part of teachers and administrators. In case of CBSE schools the scenario did not differ much. The relevant co-curricular activities should be organised in both the BSE and CBSE schools to inculcate the spirit of science and technology through scientific plays, exhibitions, etc. However, the following suggestions have been made by the educational supervisors and experts for improving the co-curricular aspects of school's science education programme:

- Organisation of science fair at least once in an academic year. It should be at state level or district level.
- Science Exhibitions at Circle level and State level.
- Debate and quiz competition on science at Circle level and State level.
- Organisation of field trips and study tours.
- Creative essay writing in science.
- Community-based science programmes should be organised to bring awareness.
- Participation of students in science club activities.

These programmes should be organised to provide first hand experience for better realisation of learners.

4.4.4 Evaluation

Evaluation is an integral part of the whole teaching-learning process. There are different types of evaluation to identify the problem areas of the students. About 7.5 percent science experts suggested to give more emphasis on objective type and objective-based test items in addition to short answer or restricted answer type items. More stress to be given on the following aspects:

- Understanding and application aspect by shifting the focus from knowledge-based test items.
- Emphasis is to be given on attitudinal and psychomoter skills.

Prevailing system of examination was defective which did not carry any appropriateness especially for the science subject. The existing system promotes the habit of cramming and regurgitate them during examinations. The creative scientific attitude of the child gets a set back. So practical-oriented objective-based questions are to be emphasised where there would be the scope for exercising convergent and divergent thinking of the learners.

4.4.5 Inspection

Inspection is an inseparable unit of entire educational edifice. Its function is to control the activities of personnel involved in teaching-learning process. As science teaching is related with experiments, laboratory works, use of aids, charts and models, etc. it needs timely inspection to get satisfactory result as regards quality of education. But in real practice the inspection is suffering from quite a lot of loopholes. The science supervisors and experts stressed the need of periodical inspection and supervision for qualitative improvement of meaningful transaction of the system. About 80 percent science experts suggested for inspection of science classes atleast once in six months.

Science Supervisors and Experts are more or less directly involved with the science education at different stages of schooling. Their suggestions and remarks for the improvement of science education especially is an important step for character and career building of the teachers and in turn students. However, the quality of prevalent curriculum, co-curriculum, laboratory facilities, examination system are questioned most of the time. For the quality improvement of science education at secondary stage needs complete renovation of the various aspects related to it. Careful preparation of text books, making curriculum life centered, improvement of evaluation system, timely orientations and refresher courses for the teachers to enable them to remain in close contact to latest development in science and technology. Inspection should be further strengthened to weed out difficulties and bottlenecks in the path of teaching-learning process.

Science education plays a key role in secondary classes as it become the last stage of education for many in our country like India. So science curriculum should be life centered, community-oriented, objective-based, performance-based and linked with the interest and need of the child to meet the demands in the real life situation.

It should be so designed to cultivate the scientific temperament and develop scientific attitude, problem-solving capacities, decision-making abilities, among the students so as to make him/her confident and competent to meet the challenges of reality of this modern time.

4.5 OPINION OF EDUCATIONISTS

An interview schedule was developed to collect the opinion of educationists across the State with the view to enrich the study.

Through the interview schedule fifteen educationists both in-service and retired from different faculties were contacted. Their views as regards to different aspects of science teaching and learning process have been placed here.

4.5.1 Science Syllabus and Contents

The main focus of formal education is syllabus of various subjects. The present syllabus and the contents of subjects are not free from deficiencies which is the prime concern of educationists of Orissa. The remarks and suggestion of educationists in this connection is note worthy and appreciable. About 80 percent educationists have suggested for integration of science subject with all other school subjects, (Its courses should be prepared to supplement to other subjects). They have further remarked, the significant difference existing between the CBSE and the BSE school's science course patterns. To minimise the differences, BSE, Orissa, syllabus should be improved through updating course pattern, evaluation system, etc. Some of the units like; computer-structure and application, prevention and cure of health hazards and recently discovered diseases such as AIDS, cancer, etc. Structure of atom, chemical bonding, photosynthesis, carbon and its compounds should be added in detail and elaborately in the existing syllabi to make it more dynamic and appropriate for the present time.

4.5.2 Methods of Teaching

Methods of teaching is of prime importance in teaching and learning process. The prevailing method of teaching needs change to make the process of education attractive and interesting. Educationists have suggested for adoption of new methods like— Activity Method, Demonstration Method, Experimentation and Discussion Method and Project Method. These should be followed by teachers and thereby enhancing student's participation as and when necessary. The local needs are to be taken into consideration while transacting science subject in secondary school classes. Physical facilities such as laboratory support materials, charts, pictorials and other laboratory equipments should be renovated or provided immediately as these materials play a key role in teaching science. As there are a good number of BSE schools run with poor laboratory or in many cases without a laboratory that worsen the science education condition in our secondary schools. Science is taught like other social sciences without experimentation and practical activity. The science teaching conditions in the CBSE schools were hopeful and better than the BSE schools. However, method of teaching should be realistic need-based and child centered. About 70 percent educationists have suggested for preparation of no-cost and low-cost teaching aids by the teachers with the help of students and avail on request to NCERT and State Government science department for providing aids and kits to promote the science teaching condition in the state.

4.5.3 Science Text Books

Science text books as like other subject text books at secondary level is the guiding pole for curricular transaction. But the present science text books of both the CBSE and the BSE syllabi are not free from comments. Crowded facts and figures and presentation of topic is not within the reach of students. While BSE courses was suffering from heavy deficiencies mostly it was theoretical instead of practical based as remarked by 80 percent educationists. Preparation of text book is a tough task as the quality of education system largely depends on it.

About 70 percent educationists sought immediate change of text book and placed suggestion for its improvement. There should be scope for appreciation, large number of examples and activities should be suitable to the age, aspiration and need of the students. Language should be simple, printing should be clear with appropriate figures, graphs, illustrations and better get up. More sample text items should be provided with the exercises for unit tests at the end of each topic. They have stresses the need to develop text books catering to the needs, interest and the requirements of the society in general and individual in particular.

4.5.4 Evaluation

Evaluation is an integral part of the education system. Many commissions and committees have examined the defects of prevailing evaluation system and suggested measures for its improvement. Evaluation of science knowledge of students at secondary level carries special emphasis as this subject has been undergone several changes frequently. The evaluation system which gives emphasis on essay type test questions promote an attitude of mechanical cramming and stereotype memorisation. As suggested by 82 percent educationists the traditional method of stereotype memorisation should be discouraged by providing due weightage to objective type questions and creative practical works in science laboratory to enhance solving capacities and decision-making abilities of students. More emphasis on application and utility of subject rather than theoretical elaboration is to be stressed. Correlated approach should be emphasised rather than disciplinary one. Written examination should be supplemented by other non-scholastic testing techniques like observation, and *viva-voce*, etc. The evaluation system with new approach should test the pupils' experience rather than mere memorisation.

4.5.5 Inspection

Inspection is an important aspect of whole education system. Timely inspection by authorities subject experts to educational institutions is highly essential to regulate the quality of curricular and co-curricular transaction. The present inspection is not free from problems which needs immediate action to improve it. Mechanism of inspection of science laboratory, teacher's performance to find out the problems involved in the process of science teaching should be evolved categorically. Some problems as mentioned discussed below:

- Indifferent attitude of authority.
- Heavy workload on the inspecting agencies.
- Avoidance and non-co-operation of school management.

Taking the above matter into consideration educationists have suggested the following measures:

- Regulate laboratory organisation and its modalities of functioning.
- Use of teaching aids, projectors, epidiascope and other technological hardwares.
- Teacher's response to the students, their specific problems and other subsidiary problems.
- Utilisation of allocated funds appropriately.
- Headmasters' co-operation and their role in inspection.

- Detailed inside and outside classroom activities should be properly inspected.
- Student's participation in co-curricular and extra-curricular activities like debate, discussion and other self-stimulating activities must be encouraged.

4.5.6 Other Suggestions

Educationists apart from their above suggestions have also recommended following aspects for quality improvement of science teaching-learning process. Involvement of community, and community need-based science topics, orientation and refresher course for teachers should be materialised to update the teaching-learning condition in science. The subject experts from NCERT, SCERT, BSE, State Government, Inspecting Officials are to inspect the institutions frequently to strengthen the science education programme.

5

Discussion and Conclusion

5.1 DISCUSSION

The data were collected from the opinions of the Headmasters and teachers serving in the secondary schools, students reading in the schools, science supervisors serving in educational circles at the district level and science experts of Board of Secondary Education, Orissa. The analysis of the opinions available from these educationists of the state shows certain converging as well as diverging trends on the problems under investigation.

The secondary schools in the State of Orissa mainly affiliated to Board of Secondary Education (BSE), Orissa located in the city of Cuttack. In all these schools the medium of instruction is Oriya, the regional language of the state. There is no provision of English medium schools affiliated to BSE, Orissa. But in the states like Tamil Nadu, Kerala, etc. even there is provision for English medium institutions affiliated to State Board of Secondary Education.

Quite a sizeable number of schools are affiliated to Central Board of Secondary Education (CBSE) located at New Delhi. Those schools are mainly Navodaya Vidyalayas, Kendriya Vidyalayas (Central Schools). Those are managed by Central autonomous bodies like Navodaya Vidyalaya Sangathan, and Kendriya Vidyalaya Sangathan respectively. Besides, many private bodies have established schools in this state which are also affiliated to Central Board of Secondary Education, New Delhi and those schools are also quite popular in this region. In all schools affiliated to Central Board of Secondary Education the medium of instruction is English. The syllabi prescribed by both the bodies are almost equivalent. Still there is a remarkable gap between the syllabi of two categories of schools particularly in Science Curriculum. There are 5235 Government and non-Government schools in the State affiliated to BSE, Orissa. There are 30 Kendriya Vidyalayas 16, Navodaya Vidyalayas and some other schools affiliated to CBSE, New Delhi.

For the purpose of this study 51 schools affiliated to BSE, Orissa and 12 affiliated to CBSE, New Delhi were selected randomly as sample and became the source of data for this study. From the demographic study of the schools it is revealed that all the CBSE affiliated schools are located in urban areas and the BSE affiliated schools are found both in rural and urban areas of the state. There are three categories of schools in the sample such as Boys' High Schools, Girls' High School and Co-education Schools where both boys and girls are usually admitted.

The enrolment of boys are much more as compared to girls in the secondary schools of Orissa. This is perhaps because of the fact that the drop out in case of girls is more predominant as compared to boys at the elementary schools of Orissa. The CBSE schools are overcrowded in comparison to BSE Schools. It might be due to the fact that there is a craze among the parents to send the children to English medium schools. Moreover, there is a common feeling that the education available in English medium schools are better than the Oriya medium schools. However, the English medium schools are quite less in number as compared to Oriya medium schools.

When the opinions provided by the Headmasters of BSE and CBSE affiliated schools were considered, it was found that there were two sets of teachers in charge of teaching science in secondary schools. One was in charge of teaching Biological Sciences having Chemistry, Botany and Zoology as optional subjects at graduation level and the other category in charge of teaching Physical Sciences having degree with Physics, Chemistry and Mathematics. It is simply because of the fact that at present context of advancement in Science and Technology there has been rapid generation of new knowledge taking place which compelled the curriculum framer to include specialised information in respective subjects in secondary school syllabus. The syllabus now enriched with higher knowledge in the field of Biological Sciences and Physical Sciences as compared to syllabus of the past. Hence, specialised teachers are required to take care of special subjects at secondary level. It is seen that more women teachers are incharge of teaching Biological Sciences as compared to Physical Sciences. This is because of the fact that more women having qualification of B.Sc. (CBZ) as compared to the B.Sc. (PCM) are attracted towards this profession due to which the presence of lady teachers in Biological Stream is more conspicuous.

Of course it is felt that Head of the institutions are quite justified in defending the science teachers of not capable of discharging their duties efficiently because of the fact that the classes of sample schools are overcrowded keeping aside the national norm of teacher-student ratio, i.e. 1:40 as prescribed by the Education Commission (1964-66) for the secondary education systems. In the present context it is widely felt that it should be 1:25, but because of population explosion the number of students are increasing very fast. Due to lack of resources and lack of political will to provide standard education it is becoming a far off dream day-by-day to provide better science education. Headmasters are also quite justified of commenting about irregular payment of salaries, non-academic preoccupation of teachers, policy of mass education and lack of teaching support materials in the class room. These facts are playing a catalytic role in deterioration of quality of science education in the present context.

As regards the in-service training programme more systematic and justified steps are to be taken. Because of rapid advancement in the field of science and pedagogy yesterday's teacher becomes redundant for today if he/she is not made up-to-date in his/her professional as well as content knowledge. Now more number of science teachers are required every year to meet the exigencies of science education. Hence, more coordinated and scientific efforts are to be taken-up to provide in-service training to each and every individual teacher. We should start coherent effort from today even otherwise it may turn to be a serious problem which we have to face in near future.

Science is one of the important subjects taught in Secondary Schools as it is based on practical demonstration. The services of auxiliary staff such as laboratory assistants and attendants apart from teachers for transacting science courses are very much essential.

The heads of institutions opined that the teachers were not able to meet the needs of students of different classes because of the following reasons:

- Classes were overcrowded.

- Teachers did not get salary in time and even salary in non-government schools was not at par with government schools.
- A sizeable number of students belong to low average group.
- Non-availability of teaching aids and other transactional facilities.

These factors act as catalyst for deterioration of mental health of teachers. In his study "Influence of Recent Life Experience as Mental Health of School Teachers". Sharma (1995) found psycho-physical strain was positively correlated with recent life experiences. Recent life experiences influenced the mental health of a teacher. Stress made the teachers predisposed to mental disorders. Male teachers are more inclined towards the mental illness.

Further the heads of the institutions were of the opinion that most of their teachers have not undergone in-service training which is a professional need. As studied and recommended by Gisler (1967) upgrading and continuous progress of teachers in the profession is very much dependent on material facilities, methodology and curriculum planning. These are some basic keys to impart successful science education.

It was also reported that some teachers availed the chances to undergo some specific in-service programmes conducted by Board of Secondary Education (BSE), Central Board of Secondary Education (CBSE), Kendriya Vidyalaya Sangathan (KVS), State Council of Educational Research and Training (SCERT) and National Council of Educational Research and Training (NCERT). But these facilities could not be available to 75.80 per cent and 48.80 per cent teachers serving in BSE and CBSE schools respectively. It was found that about 32 per cent science teachers were used to take extra classes to complete the course while 30 per cent teachers usually engaged in private tuition to help the students. It is learnt that parents/guardians sought tuition to provide additional help to their children although 78.09 per cent Headmasters did not favour the trend while some others preferred it for the reasons like:

- Science subjects need more time for conceptual clarity which is not available in regular classroom situation.
- Necessity to provide individual attention to the students.
- Home task correction.

It was revealed from the information provided by the science teachers that 37.82 per cent teachers had more than 14 years teaching experience to their credit. About 65.21 per cent teachers have undergone in-service training course (Refresher and Orientation) and attend seminars organised from time to time by different agencies to improve their teaching competencies. It was found that science teachers were able to feel that they could teach science effectively. However, 5.21 per cent science teachers focussed on problems which create hindrances in the way of effective transaction. There are many teachers who reasoned out specifically just like their heads of institutions which are mentioned here. Those were overcrowded classes, students were not competent enough to understand the subject intellectually and non-availability of salary to teachers in time. Many teachers particularly in non-government schools did not get their salary in time that too they were not paid adequately as prescribed. But on record they receive full salary though the reality was some thing different.

It is felt by the teachers that there is a craze among parents to send their children for private tuition although teachers take due care of the students in the school itself. The reasons in support of private tuition as revealed by the teachers are:

- Sufficient time is not available for effective transactional work in schools.
- Individual attention could not be given in regular classes as it is overcrowded and home assignments could not be corrected in large classes.
- Parents pressurised to take private tuition.
- Effective notes could not be given in regular classes which is a time taking programme.

However, Government has strictly prohibited tuition practices in schools. To discourage this practice every teacher has been given a teaching allowance of Rs. 100 per month in schools managed by Central Government. But this provision is not reflected in revised new pay scale introduced in 1996. No teachers in non-government schools either affiliated to CBSE or BSE enjoy this facility. This facility is also not extended by the Government of Orissa due to which no teacher of BSE affiliated schools are able to get such allowance. Rather state government frequently instructs the Headmasters to prevent private tuition practices among the teachers. But sometimes because of certain specific problems Head of the Institutions recommend the parents to send their children either for coaching classes conducted by school in or out of school hour or to send their children to some good teachers for private tuition.

Co-curricular activities are supplementary to curricular programmes. It has got definite impact to broaden the horizon of students. Patwardhan (1995) in his study found programmes through games for solving the difficulties and correcting the mistakes were quite effective. The achievement of students depend upon the location of the school, family background, surrounding of the schools and teachers. No doubt the schools in Orissa conduct co-curricular activities for students but these are not upto satisfaction. Different types of co-curricular activities are conducted at secondary level. Science exhibition in one of those activities. It is being conducted in different schools and provide scope for participation of students at Circle, State and National levels. The schools have to enforce more participation of students in such type of activities. Apart from the participation of students in co-curricular activities organised in Orissa, they also participate in the competitions organised at Birla Industrial Technical Museum (BITM), Calcutta where Eastern India Science Camp is organised annually. NCERT conducts Jawaharlal Nehru National Level Science Exhibitions on rotation in different states annually. Even BITM, Calcutta and Science Museum, Bhubaneswar organise Mobile Science Exhibition at different places on request.

It has been reported by the educational supervisors that the provision of co-curricular activities in the BSE schools was inadequate and there were also many heads of institutions and science teachers who were not interested to organise or providing scope for the students to participate in such activities due to lack of funds and lack of enthusiasm. In case of CBSE schools the scenario did not differ much. The relevant co-curricular activities should be organised in both BSE and CBSE schools to inculcate the spirit of participation in science activities so as to develop scientific attitude and scientific temper in learners.

As per the data collected from the students of both CBSE and BSE schools, there is significant difference in organising co-curricular activities by both types of schools. It was found that few CBSE schools organise study tour, field study, and project work while no sample BSE school has conducted such activities but many of them participated in science exhibitions in their school premises and in science exhibitions at District, State and National levels.

The above facts indicated that the participation in different types of co-curricular activities is not very satisfactory. Several factors might be responsible for this kind of situation. Firstly, many schools are not well communicated because of the geographical factors. Sometimes information received by the school regarding such programmes quite late because of postal delay and other factors. Secondly, as participation involves some financial commitment, many heads of the institutions do not show sufficient interest to involve the pupils and teachers. Thirdly, some teachers are not that effective to participate in the programme because of their lack of initiative to motivate the Heads of the institutions and students as well. But it is found that gradually more number of schools have started thinking positively to get involved in such programmes. Moreover, it is a very good symptom that most of the students are very much interested in joining different co-curricular activities. They feel that the theoretical classes are quite monotonous. To get relief out of the monotony, the co-curricular activities play an important role. They feel more happy and realise the utility of knowledge in real life situation. The activities really help to develop their scientific temper and attitude in right direction.

Government financial grant for science education is highly essential to ensure better standard of science teaching in secondary schools. It is found from the information of Heads of the institutions that about 76.19 per cent schools could not receive any grant while other schools received a scanty grant which is inadequate to meet the requirements of school. Only 3.17 per cent of sample schools collected money from students and others occasionally for improvement of science laboratory and materials for teaching science that too not in a very organised manner. Although allocation of more money for science teaching is widely felt yet it suffered from sheer negligence. Indifferent attitude of authority made the situation worst. There was neither public donation nor the schools were empowered to collect fund from other sources officially. The funds allocated to few schools were only for maintenance which was quite insufficient for processing and sustenance of work.

Inspection here refers to critical reviewing of one or more aspects of the school and its programmes. Historically speaking, it was introduced in the education system to enforce control and authority as an executive arm of the government. The officers-in-charge of inspection were mainly educational administrative officials who used to pay visits to schools with a view to check the work of teachers and progress of pupils as per the rules and standards prescribed by the government from time to time. It ensures the improvement of teaching standard and provide remedial measures to overcome the problem. But unfortunately inspection in present setup has suffered from ailments. But it is the immediate measure to control the situation and keep up the standard and status of school education in general and science education in particular.

As reported by the Heads of the institutions that 25 per cent BSE schools were visited by science experts from Board of Secondary Education, Orissa, Cuttack, which has appointed subject experts in science. However, government CBSE schools were supervised by the inspecting team formed by their authorities. As per the suggestions given by the 80 per cent science supervisors and experts that the inspection of science programmes should be done atleast twice in an academic year. As heads of the institutions informed around 45 per cent BSE sample schools were supervised by Inspectors of Schools once in an academic year. Their visit played an important role in improvement of academic atmosphere of the school. It was also found that 35 per cent sample schools were visited by some kind of science experts. However, the quality of prevalent curricular and co-curricular activities, laboratory facilities, examination systems are questioned with regard to its implementation and sanctity. For the quality improvement of science education at secondary level, supervision system needs complete renovation. As supervision was an integral part of the whole education system, it was not satisfactory as most of the problems were overlooked or unchanged for years together. Headmasters have the responsibility to inspect classes but in about 25 per cent BSE schools the classes were inspected by them while in all the CBSE schools the classes were inspected by the Heads of the institutions.

As per the opinion of educationists timely inspection by authorities and subject experts to educational institutions is highly essential to regulate the quality of curricular and co-curricular transactions. The present inspection is not free from problems which needs immediate attention for its improvement. An effective mechanism of inspection of science classes and teacher's performance in the process of science teaching should be evolved categorically. Some problems generally faced in the area of inspection are discussed below:

- In different attitude of authority.
- Heavy work load on the inspecting agencies.
- Avoidance and non-cooperation of school management.

Taking the above matter into consideration educationists have suggested the following measures so as to bring improvement in the science education system in Orissa:

- Organisation of laboratory activities and its effective modalities of functioning.
- Use of teaching aids, projects, epidiascope and other technological hardwares while teaching science.
- Teachers' positive response to the students' feeling and accepting sympathetically their specific problems and other subsidiary problems.
- Utilisation of allocated funds appropriately.
- Headmasters' co-operation and their constructive role in inspection.
- Students' participation in co-curricular and extra-curricular activities like debate, discussion and other self-stimulating activities to be insisted upon.
- They also stressed the involvement of community in different spheres of transaction of science activities, organisation of orientation and refresher courses for teachers for updating the teaching-learning condition of the State.

Time-table is an important aspect of formal education system. As science is a subject related to both practical and theoretical knowledge these aspects should be clearly reflected in time-table to ensure teaching and learning effectively.

It is found from the information provided by the Heads of the institutions that 87 per cent sample schools science teachers were satisfied with the number of classes available for transaction and 85 per cent teachers complete the course in due time. Even some teachers used to take extra classes to complete the course and do some revision work.

Science teachers have opined that there are about three theory classes (one each for Physics, Chemistry, Biology) and six practical classes (two each for Physics, Chemistry, Biology) for science teaching in the CBSE schools. The students were taken to laboratory in these periods for experimentation-*cum*-theory classes beyond the schedule time-table if required. However in the BSE schools students got eight science theory classes per week. There were no special periods for science practical but some enthusiastic teachers used to arrange, few practical work such as conducting experiments and demonstration in the theoretical classes. They demonstrate some activities, as opined by the students also, in course of teaching theoretical aspects of science syllabus. In both the types of schools the science classes were placed in time-table in a scattered way. No specific procedure seems to be followed in allotting the science classes during a week long time. As revealed from the response of teachers, a teacher engages in average 30 periods (Science and other subjects) in a week at secondary stages. A teacher usually demonstrate some experiments in theory classes. Students were mere spectators to these experiments demonstrated by the teachers. But in CBSE affiliated schools because of the provision of laboratory class in their time-table, students work in laboratory and received first hand experience under the supervision of teachers.

But the sample teachers of both the schools expressed their feelings to have more number of periods in science subjects specifically per week. The placement of science periods in time-table perhaps is not able to find justice because of the following factors in school plant as they opined:

- Non availability of space in school building.
- Paucity of funds to purchase necessary apparatus and equipment for students.
- Presence of too many subjects to be accommodated in the time-table.
- Lack of sufficient science teachers in school.

Course content and methodology occupies an important place in curriculum transaction. There were many discussions resulting in revision of the courses at secondary school stage in general and science course in particular. It is known that curricular materials are related directly to the contents prescribed in syllabus.

It is found from the information of Heads of the institutions that science course is changing from time to time to introduce innovations and development in the different branches of science. The syllabus is being well framed with important materials as assessed by 87 per cent Headmasters while 13 per cent of them sought change in the syllabus. But as many as 80 per cent of BSE sample teachers felt that the content of science course was appropriate and relevant to the needs of time, society and students. As it has been reported earlier that teachers could complete the courses in time and in many cases science teachers also had to take extra classes for such purpose. Many teachers claim that they face problems because of some difficult content and non-availability of teaching aids. The science course content had got enough applied reflection of the facts in real life situation. Many teachers were of the opinion that the curricula prescribed by BSE and CBSE authorities though did not satisfy all the principles of curriculum construction still there were some considerable effort of taking care of the principles of utility, variety, need, relevance, readiness and flexibility, etc. Still they recommended for regular revision of the curricula to make it effective and upto-date. Few of these problems indicated by the science teachers against the existing course are discussed below:

- Number of period allotted per week for science teaching was insufficient.
- Many topics have higher level of difficulty.
- Over loaded syllabus.
- Requirement of extensive use of teaching aids as per the content.

Science teachers of both BSE and CBSE schools have given their positive and negative remarks. They denied the presence of irrelevant content matter in the text book. They have supported the presence of many useful and important topics, presence of upto-date information about modern development, adequacy of content on applied aspect of science, and different branches of science proportionately represented in science curriculum. They admit the presence of factual mistakes of the content matter in the text book. The sample teachers are having favourable opinion about the presence of different branches of science. They say that more emphasis has been granted to Physics, Chemistry, Biology,

Agriculture and Animal Husbandry. They expressed satisfaction over the sequential distribution/presentation of different streams in both the syllabi.

So far as the students of both the sample schools are concerned they too have expressed their satisfaction with the syllabi. But many of BSE school students were not satisfied with the pictorial presentation of content matter in their text books while the CBSE students felt somewhat better about it. They were of the opinion that contents of science text books were well selected but they were not able to completely depend on it. The sample students had to be dependent on some outside books for better learning to substantiate the deficiency they found from the text book. The text book was not sufficient for teaching the entire content of syllabus.

It was also observed that sometimes students used to take the help of guide and key book notes for their study. However, the science supervisor/educationists informed that the syllabus in general and science syllabus in particular are not free from comments. Overcrowded facts and figures and presentation of topics is not within the reach of students. BSE course was suffering from heavy deficiencies as mostly it has theoretical representation rather than practical orientation as reported by 80 per cent of sample educationists. Preparation of text book is a tough task as the quality of education system largely depends on it.

About 70 per cent educationists sought an immediate change of text book and placed a few suggestions for its improvement. There should be ample scope for providing sufficient examples and activities, content should be suitable to the need and aspiration of the students language should be simple, printing should be clear with appropriate figures, graphs and illustrations and different types of sample evaluation item should be provided with the exercises for unit tests at the end of each topic. The findings of other researches also supported the view about the dynamic character of curricula. The evidences indicate that regular review and modifications are essential to make the curricula effective (Sing, 1977, Pradhan, 1978).

As reported by Heads of the institutions, method of teaching plays a key role to transact syllabus. Teachers have been provided with full autonomy as regards the use of teaching strategies, approaches and designs. They are supposed to evolve their unique strategies to deal effectively with the exigencies they faced during the transactional period. Science is a practical-oriented process-based subject. It needs upto-date flexibility in methodology. However 40 per cent Headmasters have expressed their dissatisfaction as regards methodology used by their teachers. Teachers just adopted most unscientific lecture method which made science teaching-learning monotonous and difficult, while 58.73 per cent sample school Headmasters expressed their satisfaction on the methods adopted by their teachers. However, it was found that about 72 per cent Headmasters of sample schools, were satisfied with the performance of the science teachers working with them.

A science teacher has got his own teaching style and at the same time each learner has his/her unique learning technique. In reality no subject is dry or difficult which creates problem for learners. The teachers makes the subject interesting for learners because of his/her acrobatics exhibited while interacting with the learners. However, the responses of BSE affiliated school teachers revealed that usually they follow lecture, discussion and seldom demonstration-*cum*-discussion and observation methods while transacting science curricula. But CBSE teachers employ laboratory, project and assignment methods in addition to the methods followed by their counter parts in BSE schools. But it was found that mostly lecture method dominated the course of interaction by the sample teachers irrespective of the type of schools. The project and assignment methods were used in CBSE schools at times as it was the requirement of their course of interaction. It was also revealed from the information supplied by science teachers that majority of sample schools did not subscribe any journals in the field of content and pedagogy of science even though the teachers were interested in it.

As informed by the educationists there is need to change the prevailing method of teaching to make education attractive and interesting. Educationists have recommended different methods of teaching at secondary level such as activity method, demonstration method, experimentation and discussion method and project method. Physical facilities such as laboratory, support materials like charts, pictorials and other laboratory equipments should be renovated immediately. As a large number of BSE schools have no laboratories or are very poorly equipped and science is taught like other social science subjects without experimentation and practical activity, the method of teaching should be realistic, need-based and child centered. However, 70 percent educationists have suggested for preparation of no-cost and low-cost teachings aids by the teachers with the help of the students. But in reality in both the types of schools lecture method is followed which is considered as a more weak method of teaching. San Sanwal and Suri (1995) in their study revealed that the students taught through programmed learning materials achieved significantly higher than those taught through lecture method for chemistry teaching in Secondary School.

Educational supervisors have emphasised the use of audio-visual aids and upto-date methods of teaching like demonstration, experiment method, etc. It could develop interest among the learners to get knowledge of science through the use of hardwares like chalkboard, sophisticated computer, television, tape recorder, radio, etc. These could have massive use in the classroom to ensure better learning by students. About 89 per cent science experts have expressed their concern over the poor use of teaching aids as regards time and context both.

The development of science and technology has direct impact on the student in classroom. Use of teaching aids encourages students for better way of learning in his classroom. It was also revealed that there are schools where authorities are indifferent to provide upto-date facilities and laboratories. The difference as regards such facilities between the BSE and CBSE schools were quite significant. They emphasised in the appointment of laboratory assistants and creation of Botanical gardens in the school premises.

The students of both BSE and CBSE schools have expressed satisfaction over the science course and content and the difference of course between two schools are not significant. BSE school students are not satisfied with the pictorial and graphical presentation of topic. It is also informed by the CBSE school students that they have to rely on other subsidiary books like key books, notebooks or refresher books alongwith the text books prescribed by the both CBSE and BSE authorities.

Science teaching is an important task before the teachers as it needs infrastructural facilities such as laboratory, laboratory equipments, chemicals, teaching aids, etc. Renovation of laboratory facilities is essential for making science education interesting and impressive at secondary level. Mohany (1987) emphasised the equipments and laboratory facilities for effective science education.

It was revealed from the information supplied by the science teachers, heads of the institutes and students that majority of CBSE affiliated schools had separate science room/laboratory for regular instructional work. But most of the BSE schools have no such facilities, these rooms or laboratories have long wall black board, demonstration table, permanent demonstration charts facilities and some other facilities to use as and when necessary. Permanent water supply, electric connection, provision of gas cylinders to conduct experiments, exhaust fan and well equipped working table fitted with water basins to be used by the students are integral part of a science laboratory in schools. But in few BSE schools such facilities are available. But in other schools transaction of science curricular activities were being conducted in regular classrooms just like the other subjects, as a result of which science teaching become theoretical and monotonous. Very rarely some enthusiastic science teachers carry aids and support materials related to the topic to the class and demonstrate some experiments. About 35.29 per cent of BSE sample schools do not have separate room to store science materials. The science materials were stored in some almirah and kept in room alongwith other materials. In many schools even the science kit boxes remain unopened from the beginning itself and the reason stated by the teachers was lack of space in the school building to display which is to some extent a fact also.

As informed by science teachers no sample schools of both BSE and CBSE affiliated had separate science library. But the science books are kept in general library alongwith other books. Almost all the schools agreed that most of the students could not develop scientific attitude as teaching science would not be made effective what so ever might be the reasons. About 96.07 per cent of BSE schools did not subscribed regularly to any science magazine or journals to be used by the teachers and students, while 58 per cent CBSE schools subscribe to science magazine and journals.

Schools where the audio-visual aids are not used have given the following reasons:

- The teaching aids are not available in the school.

- If available are not sufficient.
- Lack of scope to use aids in class-room situation.

Heads of the institutions of different schools have opined that the science teachers are quite capable of using teaching aids but they are helpless because of non-availability of such materials. Few of the ambitious teachers use low-cost and no-cost teaching aids while teaching science. But majority teachers tried to manage to teach with least aids and often without teaching aids. Another very important facts has revealed from the Headmasters that 32 per cent teachers believe that it is difficult to complete the course because of the extensive use of teaching aids. There is significant difference in availability and use of teaching aids between the CBSE and BSE affiliated schools. However, charts related the subjects like Physics, Botany, Zoology and Chemistry are available to some extent in all the sample schools. Others required teaching aids such as Globe, Maps Boards for displaying scientific articles are available to some extent in all the schools. Audio aids such as radio, tape recorder, slide projector microscope, epidiascope and audio-visual aids like television, film projector were available in some of the CBSE schools only.

Sharma and others (1995) in their study made a list of administrative, academic and personal problems as faced by principals, teachers and students of Navodaya Vidyalayas of Rajasthan. The existing problems included shortage of reading rooms and unfavourable policy of appointment, salaries of teachers, unsatisfactory teacher co-operation in running schools, late receipt of financial grants, shortage of teachers and science teachers were not punctual, shortage of teaching materials and teaching aids. Most of the time principals were busy in supervision work, meeting with parents, solving the problems of students, looking into hostel mess matters for self-improvement.

It seems barring a few CBSE schools no sample school have science club. But those who have science club are in disorganised form. No sample school had Eco-club. The reasons were mentioned below:

- No special fund is available for Eco-club or science club activities.
- Neither the teachers nor the students were interested in such activities and some teachers were of the opinion that those were unnecessary headache to the teachers' concerned.

- No reward/appreciation to the teacher's involved in such activities.

From the above discussion it is clear that irrespective of affiliation either to CBSE or BSE the sample schools are not well equipped as regards infrastructural facilities. Government agencies, non-Government organisations and management bodies of the school in Orissa schould initiate actions to as regards science teaching-learning condition. Science teaching without adequate infrastructural facilities play a little role in maintaining scientific temper and developing scientific attitude among the students, earning knowledge about science subjects is certainly not enough but realising utility of the knowledge in real life situation has got utmost importance in the life of a learner. Particularly the condition of the BSE affiliated schools creates a serious concern. The department of education should take special care for elevation of the condition. Rather the schools should be permitted to develop an education fund with the approval of the competent authority and they must be accountable for it. Different sources of community should be encouraged to donate generously through the standard means. Even the income tax rule should be applied generously by for those who contribute for the said purpose. For better utilisation of the fund the community and school plant should work hand in hand.

Evaluation is a process of appraising the nature of evidence about the performance of pupils in a particular subject. It's main aim is to improve the quality of education process and individual child as a whole. It measures the performances of a pupil in scholastic and non-scholastic areas. Evaluation of knowledge of student in science at secondary level carries special emphasis as this curriculum has undergone several changes frequently. The evaluation system which gives emphasis on essay type test questions, speaks about only mechanical cramming and stereotype memorization at this level. As suggested by 80 per cent educationists, the traditional method of stereotype memorisation should be discouraged by providing adequate weightage of objective type test items and creative practical work in science laboratory to enhance the problem-solving capacities and decision-making abilities of the students. More emphasis on application and utility of subject rather than theoretical elaboration is to be stressed. Correlated approaches should be emphasised rather than disciplinary one. Written examination should be supplemented by non-testing techniques like observation, and *viva-voce* etc. The evaluation system with new approach should test the pupil's experience rather than mere memorization.

However, many of the sample science teachers, in average could find difficulty in assessing the non-scholastic competence of the students. As many as 91.78 per cent teachers in average pointed out that they could not face any difficulty in preparing test items which was doubtful. It was found that the process of evaluation posed a challenging task in front of the working teachers. As per the opinion of the science teachers the assignments and home tasks are integral part of the total formal education process. However, only 20 per cent and 68 per cent of students of BSE and CBSE affiliated schools respectively opined that home tasks were verified by the school teachers. As reported by the students almost no BSE school conduct monthly science test but even if conducted by a few, these tests were not seriously taken. Follow-up actions were not geared in any case to rectify the defects detected by the use of these tests while many of the students opined that teachers checked thoroughly the assignments submitted by them and used to give necessary remarks as corrective measures in respect of the CBSE sample schools. Majority of CBSE schools organised monthly tests on science and informed to parents for necessary action at their end.

This poor handling of evaluation in both the types of school is not a good sign in our secondary education scenario. Now-a-days in schools most of the teachers are not very much interested to get involved in regular process of evaluation. Even they are not well equipped with processes of continuous and comprehensive evaluation though it is a big cry of the day. Our teacher education programme should be reorganised and special in-service programme on evaluation should be conducted stressing sufficiently the technique and processes of continuous and comprehensive evaluation. This faulty system of public examination is not able to provide proper certification to the students about his/her performance due to which present day students are facing identity crisis after he/she passes out from education system. The learner after completing their career have to face this identity crisis not because of their fault but due to inherent problem of the system. No where they are going to be identified because of their certificates. The certificates become a source of eligibility but not the proof of their competence or expertise. Though the products have got lot of potentialities, it is not properly nurished from the beginning. Rather an effective system of evaluation should be enforced right from the beginning of elementary level so that it can take a better shape at secondary level. Let there be some weightage whatever teacher says about the past, present and future for his/her learner. When both the types of schools are considered it becomes evident that in the BSE affiliated school the evaluation system is still poorer as compared to the CBSE affiliated schools. It might be due to the fact that in inspection and supervision system is somewhat better enforced in the latter schools than the former, though it has not come up to the mark of expectation. It may be said in this context that if the inspection and supervision system could be strengthened perhaps the evaluation process in the schools might be geared up to some extent.

5.2 CONCLUSION

The study "A critical appraisal of science education programme at the secondary level" is an attempt to reflect and discover facts about the science education system at secondary level in an educationally backward State, i.e. Orissa. The overall literacy percentage and women education programme do not show any satisfactory progress of education in the state. Apart from emphasis laid down by the government for spread of universal elementary education, the importance of secondary education is realised in every quarters of the society. As secondary education acts as a link between elementary education and higher education and it becomes the turning point in the career and life of students. Science education particularly has greater implications in the social life and academic career of the child. The condition of teaching-learning situation of science education at secondary level has been unfolded to a great extent through this study. It has been tried best to explore the causes and consequences of science education.

Science education pertains to the overall performance of a group of personnel such as science teachers, headmasters, laboratory assistants, supervisors, experts and other related individuals. Besides the other conditions like laboratory conditions, i.e. availability of space, room equipments, chemicals, etc. influence very much the student performances. It is found from the date that quite a sizeable number of schools are affiliated to Central Board of Secondary Education (CBSE), New Delhi. Those schools are mainly Navodaya Vidyalayas, Kendriya Vidyalayas (Central Schools) which are managed by central autonomous bodies like Navodaya Vidyalaya Sangathan and Kendriya Vidyalaya Sangathan respectively. Besides many private bodies have established schools in this state which are affiliated to CBSE, New Delhi and these schools are quite popular in this region. In all schools affiliated to CBSE the medium of instruction is English. These are generally urban-based schools. Secondly, there are several schools affiliated to Board of Secondary Education (BSE) Orissa, Cuttack. Those schools are purely managed by Government and some are non-government schools spread all over Orissa in rural and urban areas. Those are in the form of Girls' High Schools, Boys' High Schools and Co-educational Institutions. The courses transacted here are in the regional language, Oriya. These schools have numerical supremacy over the CBSE schools in the state.

It is now felt after conducting the study that in-service teacher training programme is highly essential to enhance the professional competence of teachers and Headmasters.

However, there are a number of problems responsible for decreasing the professional interest among the teachers as opined by heads of the institutions few of those are overcrowded classes, salary and delayed payment, apathetic attitude of administrative machinery and other reasons arising out of place of posting. The heads of the institutions also disclosed that although in-service training is urgent need of a teacher, most of them have not got scope to attend even a single in-service training programme which are usually organised by Board of Secondary Education, Kendriya Vidyalaya Sangathan, Navodaya Vidyalaya Sangathan, NCERT and other agencies in this region.

There are a number of science teachers (32 per cent) who take extra classes for completing the course while 30 per cent science teachers are in favour of giving private tuition to the students as it is the demand of the students and their parents. However, CBSE affiliated schools (excepting some public schools) have banned this practice by offering a teaching allowance. But this provision has not been reflected in new scale of pay. But in BSE affiliated school although government has several times warned to ban the practice but that is in vain. The classes are over-crowded and lack of proper laboratory facilities usually add to confusion of the students. Even sometime heads of institutions direct the students to undergo private tuition for their betterment.

Co-curricular activities play an important role in development of child's character and academic career. It is a part and parcel of curricular activities. The condition of co-curricular activities in secondary schools are far from satisfaction. Both CBSE and BSE affiliated schools are to improve the standard and spirit of participation of schools particularly in co-curricular activities so as to develop scientific temper among the students and diverting the potentiality of students in right direction.

The root of every problem is financial constrain in this region. Most of the heads of institutions said that their schools were not able to receive any type of grant. Few schools receive a scanty grant. There is no provisions to collect money in the form of donation from the parents of the students for the development of science education, but a few private schools collect nominal fees for the said purpose. Government grant is not sufficient to meet the requirement of laboratory chemicals and equipments, etc. So provision of money should be made at government level to ensure good laboratory for the secondary schools and or the schools should be empowered to collect their own resources.

Inspection ensures the quality of teaching-learning situation. However, it is found that the inspection and supervision of these schools are not regular. As most of science supervisors and experts said there must be inspection of school twice in an academic year. Head of the institutions should also given attention to this aspect of the administration as it is related to quality improvement of education. It has already been suggested by many educationists to create an inspecting wing of BSE, Orissa by appointing more educational experts and science supervisors. The involvement should be ensured to improve the overall standard of education.

Although many teachers are satisfied with existing syllabus particularly in science course, there is a wide demand to change the courses of the study to make it befitting to the situation. It has been suggested to prepare curriculum on the basis of utility, variety, need, relevance, readiness and flexibility to meet the emerging need of the society. It is also claimed that many topics have higher level of difficulty which require the use of exclusive teaching aids and exposure in laboratory and this might improve the scenario to some extent.

Many educationists sought to bring about improvement in science text book and prepare it with utmost care to highlight the needs and aspirations of the students. There should be simple language, illustration and more exercise should be given to develop problem-solving attitude of the pupil and regular review of the book is also emphasised. To overcome the problems of teachers as regards the transactional mode, quality resource books for teachers should be evolved by taking the help of working teachers and content experts.

Teaching is a personal and creative activity of the teachers but every student has his/her own way of learning. It is found that CBSE school teachers are better in their adoption of different methods of teaching. They have the scope of using demonstration-*cum*-discussion, project and assignment methods which could be emphasised in BSE schools also.

Regarding the science-related books, journals and magazines it is found that many schools do not subscribe to any journal. They confined their study to the text and few other substandard books. The condition of library as a whole is precarious and the science books and journals are not available easily. It is also noticed that there are no laboratory facilities and other teaching facilities in majority schools. Few enthusiastic teachers take initiative of their own to use low-cost and no-cost aids to involve students in the process. Lack of teaching aids such as radio, television, tape recorder cause several teaching-learning problems in many BSE schools. The CBSE affiliated schools have separate science room, laboratory for instructional work regularly. These rooms have requisite facilities to demonstrate and some other aids necessary as and when required. The science teaching become very theoretical in absence of science laboratory. However, in many BSE schools the kit boxes, have remained unopened and the reason as stated is due to lack of space and other facilities.

Evaluation has always been emphasised as an important measure to test the performance of the students. There are many complains both in the BSE and the CBSE schools to change the pattern of examination. It is found that the BSE schools are inferior to the CBSE schools in the sincerity to test the student performance through formative and summative evolution. So there is an urgent need to renovate the system of examination to make it more psychological and scientific. There is a peculiar trend, it is felt, which is gaining momentum in the field of evaluation more in urban set up than the rural one. That is after public examination concludes, many influential parents use their means to influence the examiners to manipulate the grade point scored by their children. Though it is very difficult to have documentary evidence in support of this kind of activities, still some worth-while measures should be adopted to check this tendency. Even the parents of high achievers are not far behind in the race. One could find a point here and that is the photocopies of best twenty answer papers of each subject could be circulated to schools so as to put it in the form of model answer scripts. This might serve two purposes, i.e. all students will get an ideal about the technique of writing answers in a better way and the influential parents might be discouraged to influence the examiners.

6

Summary and Recommendations

6.1 SUMMARY

6.1.1 Introduction

We are living now in an age rapid changes. Science is playing a dominant role in bringing about these changes. It is no exaggeration to say that, at present science influences every field of our activities. The technological advances have explored and multiplied the possibilities of affording sustenance and comforts to human beings. Thus from cradle to grave scientific discoveries and inventions have inextricably woven themselves into the fabric of human existence.

Now, it becomes very essential to be in possession of some basic knowledge of science on the part of each individual. One encounters with innumerable events and objects regularly in his/her social and natural environment which regulates the daily life. To understand these a bit manipulation of the basic knowledge in science is the prerequisite. The water we drink, the air we breath, the food we take, the shelter we undertake, the commodities we transport, the clothing we wear and in all sphere our life we face a lot of problems. To get solution to these we are bound to take assistance of knowledge which has got strong basis of science. Considering these aspects, science has been included in the school curriculum even from elementary stage so as to make human being an efficient one. In new pattern of 10 + 2 Education System, science is one of the major subjects to be taught in secondary schools. Hence, the school as well as the science teacher have immense responsibility in the changed situation particularly in teaching of science. It is proper to know the perspectives and problems of science education in our State, i.e.

the state of Orissa. Hence, it was attempted to have "A Critical Appraisal of Science Education at the Secondary Level".

6.1.2 Objectives of the Study

The objectives of the study were as detailed:

(i) To make a survey of the existing provisions and facilities available for organising Science Education programme in secondary schools of Orissa.
(ii) To find out the lacunae and deficiencies in the Science Education programme which is in vogue to meet the requirement of Secondary School students.
(iii) To identify the strengths and good practices in the system.
(iv) To pool the views and suggestions of the Teachers, Supervisors and Educationist in order to suggest remedies for removal of the deficiencies.
(v) To recommend the measures for improving the Science Education programme in Secondary Schools.

6.1.3 Delimitation of the Study

The problem which is selected to be investigated is quit a vast one which requires enormous time, energy and financial support. Keeping these constraints in view the study has been delimited to the following:

- All the sample schools were either affiliated to Board of Secondary Education, Orissa, Cuttack or Central Board of Secondary Education, New Delhi.
- The Boys' schools, Girls' schools and Co-education schools of urban and rural background are included in the study.
- The study is restricted only to Science Education Programme conducted in the secondary schools of Orissa by the year 1995.

6.1.4 Methodology

6.1.4.1 Sample

The schools were selected on the basis of stratified random sampling. The sample thus was the systematic representation of all the Secondary Schools spread over nine districts of Orissa such as Balasore, Bolangir, Bargarh, Cuttack, Ganjam, Khurda, Puri, Sundargarh and Sambalpur. The distribution of sample has been indicated in the diagram given in Fig. 6.1.

Fig. 6.1: Showing Distribution of Sample Schools

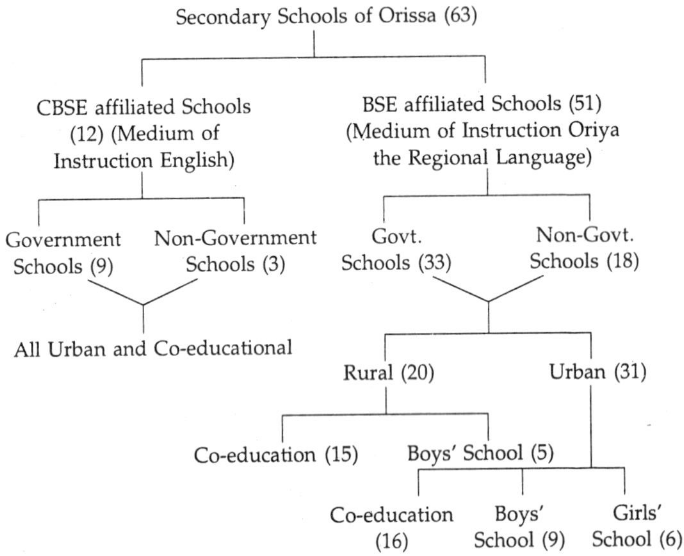

However all 12 CBSE schools were situated in urban areas and all were co-educational type. English is the medium of instruction in CBSE schools whereas Oriya, the regional language is the medium of instruction in BSE affiliated schools.

Data were collected from different personnel like Headmasters, Science Teachers and Students of higher classes of the schools, Science Supervisors working in the office of the Circle Inspectors of Schools and Educationists who were concerned about science education. Altogether 63 Headmasters, 230 Science Teachers (180 from BSE schools and 50 from CBSE schools), 500 Students (400 from BSE schools and 100 from CBSE schools), 15 Science Supervisors and Experts and 15 Educationists constituted the sample.

6.1.4.2 Tools and Techniques

A questionnaire was developed with great care to elicit information from the Headmasters about individual schools, the institutional conditions for teaching science, infrastructural facilities available at secondary level, information regarding management of school, co-curricular activities usually conducted, information regarding the finance, inspection system, time-table allotment, course content and methods of teaching. In the tool scope was provided to elicit suggestions and criticism on the existing science education programme which is in vogue in the state.

A questionnaire for the Science Teacher was developed which had two sections. The first section of the questionnaire consists of nine broad items and each time has five to seven sub-items the items were about general information about the teachers' concerned, time table, science room facilities, science laboratory, library, teaching aids facilities, curricular and co-curricular activities, home assignments to students, evaluation process and standard of text books. The first section of the questionnaire provides information as regards to the status of science education in secondary schools whereas the second one reveals specific information as regards to the problems faced by science teachers in the school during teaching and learning situation.

Another questionnaire was developed for students belonging to both CBSE and BSE affiliated schools. Information was collected with the help of the questionnaire about different aspects such as locality of the school, science teachers, their attitude towards students, science room facilities, laboratory condition, library facility and participation in co-curricular activities, etc.

An opinionnaire for science supervisors and experts was developed seeking information as evaluation, co-curricular activities, inspection of science programmes and suggestions for their improvement.

An interview schedule for educationist was developed to elicit remarks on science syllabus, improvement, of the programme, methods of teaching, physical facilities available for science practical, co-curricular activities and above all the inspection and evaluation process which were in vogue in the state.

6.1.4.3 Data Collection

The survey technique was adopted in collecting data. After the development of Questionnaires, Opinionnaire and Interview Schedule for the target groups, data were collected first hand by establishing direct contact with all the respondents concerned.

6.1.5 Findings

The major findings of the study were as follows:

- There was dearth of trained science teachers in both physical and natural sciences in the schools as a result of which interchange of teaching of the subjects by the teachers become the common practice.
- Although sections of different classes have been opened in view of increasing number of students but the number of teachers remained the same.
- Lack of auxiliary staff was very common among the secondary schools.
- There is no science laboratory in most of the BSE schools and few of the CBSE schools.
- Chemical and other consumable materials were only met 40% of laboratory requirements. But all the secondary schools of both the categories schools had some equipments, chemicals and science apparatus.
- Teaching aids were not adequately available in majority schools. Of course, some enthusiastic teachers used self-prepared low-cost and no-cost teaching aids but these were not sufficient.
- Although there were Circle level, State level, and National level competitions in Debate, Essay, Quiz and Science Exhibition, etc. but hardly few schools participated in the same, the reason being lack of communication, delayed information and negligent attitude of educational administrators and school personnel.
- There was provision for inspection of institutions. In BSE schools science teaching is normally inspected by Inspectors of Schools and Science Experts from Board of Secondary Education, Orissa, Cuttack. Government CBSE schools were inspected by the supervisors appointed by their competent authorities. However in some non-government schools classes were inspected by the members of managing committee who were not competent. There was no equal parameter of quality checking and supervisory work was unsatisfactory because of the negative attitude of the personal involved.

- There were 32 theory periods available for a teacher per week for teaching science in BSE schools and absolutely no scope for conducting practical work in the time-table while a science teacher in CBSE schools got 18 theory classes with one practical class for each science branch, i.e. physics, chemistry and biology per week. It indicated the work load variation in both the categories of school.
- Course, content and methodology of science teaching were almost equivalent in both CBSE and BSE schools. Methods followed by the science teachers in both the categories of schools were mostly lecture method and invariably they used text book while teaching. Rarely demonstration-*cum*-discussion and other better dynamic methods were used by the science teachers in schools.
- Deficiencies in teaching and auxiliary staff found in both BSE and CBSE affiliated schools. In the BSE school science teachers are sometimes transferred and an arts teacher substituted him. It was due to the defective transfer policy. There was lack of adequate science hands which caused serious hurdles in science teaching in many schools.
- Even some teachers do not get monthly salary regularly as they have been adjusted without financial sanction in the budget of the State.
- There were no special science library in some schools of both the categories. Hardly half of the sample CBSE schools subscribed to science magazines but these were quite insufficient
- There were no BSE schools having Botanical gardens excepting few CBSE affiliated schools.
- There were no Science clubs and Eco-clubs in sample secondary schools.
- The participation of science teachers in co-curricular activities were far from satisfactory.
- In the CBSE courses there was provision of assessment of assignments in the evaluation system but the same provision was not in the BSE schools.
- There was not provision of monthly test in the BSE affiliated schools but most of the CBSE schools conduct monthly tests to assess the achievement of the students.

6.2 RECOMMENDATIONS

After a detail study of secondary school science education problems in Orissa the following measures are recommended for its improvement.

6.2.1 Qualifications of a Science Teacher

- A secondary school science teacher is required to have a post-graduate degree not simply the graduate degree in science to meet the requirements of present day science curriculum.
- In-service teacher training should be compulsory for all science teaches. A teacher must attend an Orientation Course once in every five years to refresh his/her knowledge in content as well as techniques of teaching.
- An In-service Training Cell must be in operation under the disposal of Inspector of Schools at the circle level to keep liaison with organisations conducting in-service teacher training and the teachers who are to attend it. The function of cell should be to regulate in-service training of the teachers within the circle. Stringent action should be taken against the teachers failing to attend the training without sufficient reasons. A science teacher should be motivated to attend seminars, workshops, symposiums and present papers of his desires.
- Some teachers are opting to attend such courses repeatedly. There should be regulations to control the same.
- Teachers are to be motivated to conduct action research programme and make use of the result in the working situations. This has to be monitored by the above mentioned cell.
- Present transfer policy should be modified so that a science teacher of physical science or natural science can be transferred as per the requirement of the school just not as per the requirement of the teacher concerned or whim of the authority. It must be such that teaching of the school would not suffer from lack of science teacher at any cost.
- A separate cadre for science teachers need be formed to ensure better job opportunity and attract good and talented persons for science teaching.

- There must be an auxiliary staff for handling science laboratory as it is a practical subject. The number of this type of staff may be commensurated with the student's strength and sections opened in the school. They will be incharge of store/science room and laboratory.
- An academic diary should be maintained under the headings of date period, class, practicals, progress made and homework given by the science teacher.

6.2.2 Infrastructure Facilities

Laboratory

A laboratory-*cum*-science room is the basic requirement of the school. Steps in this direction should be taken. In science room charts, diagrams, graphs are to be displayed, fixed and laboratory equipments and chemicals are to be stored as per requirement.

Library

Attention must be given to up-grade library condition keeping in view of the needs of students and teachers. There should be reference books, magazines, journals for updating teacher's knowledge. Science books can be kept in general library but its importance should be realised by the students and teachers.

6.2.3 Teaching-Learning Process

Methods of Teaching

The different methods that are to be practised in schools are as follows:

Lecturer Method, Demonstration Method, etc.

Lecture-*cum*-demonstration method, observation-*cum* discussion problem solving, project-method, laboratory method topic and assignment methods.

Out of all the methods lecture-*cum*-demonstration, observation-*cum*-discussion methods are very much recommended for science teaching in our condition. In these methods the teacher goes on demonstrating what he says through charts, graphs, models, experiments and cinematography, etc. Lecture without demonstration a film having sound without picture and demonstration without caption.

6.2.4 Audio-visual Aids in Teaching

Now it is recommended that the audio-visual aids like T.V., Cassette recorder, projectors, Cinematography, V.C.R. and Radio sets should be provided to each school and be incorporated in teaching methods in all the secondary schools. Through these the demonstrations to the students are made more attractive, acceptable, lively and understandable. The students not only easily comprehend the content but also able to remember it better for longer duration. The creative potentiality of the child is also enhanced because of it.

(a) Use of TV

Educational Technology can be of maximum useful in the training of teachers to improve quality of teaching. The Central Institutes of Educational Technology of NCERT, New Delhi at the national level and the State Institute of Educational Technology, at the state level are expected to provide necessary expertise and know-how for effective utilisation, evaluation and feedback of ETV programmes. The INSAT is a challenging national project and its experiments with television programmes is capable of providing new light and insight into the viewing problems and conditions of the rural audience. Maximum use of it must be ensured.

(b) Film Shows

Scientific films are now produced by expert agencies and a good deal of research is being done before producing a scientific film. The duration is usually 1 and 1/2 hours. They can demonstrate many things in a much simple way. Films can demonstrate the processes of formation of rain, formation of snow, change of season, circulation of blood and heart functioning, occurrence of solar and lunar eclipses, etc. in more details which no teacher can do in a classroom by means of pictures and charts and black-board work.

The films should be shown weekly in large congregation. The shows should be followed by classroom discussion.

6.2.4 Science Fairs, Exhibitions and Science Club Activities

Every school should organise science fairs at least once a year. The programme should include exhibits prepared by the students. Talks by experts, film shows on scientific topics debate and discussions, music shows, scientific plays, Quiz, etc. can also be organised. Both the teacher and pupils should cooperate and contribute towards the success of such fairs. Every school must encourage science club activities and these activities are to be assessed at State level.

6.2.5 Science Museum

It is very much desirable that every school should have a science museum of its own. The science teacher should encourage the students to collect materials of scientific interest and improvise some apparatus. The collection of materials relating to different branches of science and a systematic arrangement of the same should be on the basis of a co-operative and active endeavour of the teachers and the students alike.

6.2.6 Excursion and Tours

Learning in the classroom can not be sufficient for a student of modern times. So excursion and visits and field trips to different places of scientific importance should be organised annually to give an opportunity to the participants to get direct and practical learning experiences in an interesting manner. Science teacher must arrange tours to Radio Station, Telephone Exchange, Gardens, Factories, Planetorium which will supplement class-room instruction. The science teacher must advise the students to collect information and note them accurately for their study to develop the habit of correct observation and recording.

6.2.7 Modification of Science Syllabus

Science syllabus needs to be thoroughly revised and new topics are to be included taking into consideration of the resources available in the schools and the needs of children in every three years.

6.2.8 Improving Supervision Work

Inspection and supervision of science teaching in the school is very essential for improving the teaching of science. The inspecting personnel should inspect the items like Science Teacher's Record, Time Table, Teacher's Diary, Scheme of Work, Note Books of Students, Laboratory Equipments and Stock Register, Science Club Activities, Science Museum, Science Library.

There should be a separate science expert post in every Inspectorate, i.e. in every educational circle in the rank of Deputy Inspector. He is needed to be incharge of supervision of science classes regularly in the circle. He may be assisted by the present science supervisor available in the office of the Inspector of schools.

6.2.9 Upgradation of the Text Books

The review of existing text books is felt very essential. Workshops are to be organised to develop suitable text books and agencies like NCERT, SCERT, etc. should take leadership in this regard. Both working teachers and subject experts need be involved in the programme of upgrading text book.

6.3 SUGGESTIONS FOR FURTHER STUDIES

The following intensive and extensive studies are suggested for further research:

1. There should be special study to be conducted on the prevailing curriculum and laboratory conditions separately to reveal the situation microscopically.
2. Science Education in Secondary Schools of Tribal areas can be taken separately to know their interest and attitude to deal with the problems elaborately.
3. A critical assessment of Evaluation in Science Education programme can be taken up.
4. Study of attitude and aptitude of science teachers and critical analysis of their qualification, working conditions in the secondary schools of Orissa is very much needed.
5. The cost effective analysis of science education programme in the state is very much essential.

Bibliography

Aggarwal, J.C. (1975). *Educational Research, An Introduction,* New Delhi: Arya Book Depot.

Aranha, J. (1988). *An Experiment in Mastery Learning in Science.* Ph.D. Education, Baroda: The Maharaja Sayajirao University.

Arora, S.K. (1986). *In Buch, M.B. (1997). Fifth Survey of Educational Research (1988-92).* New Delhi: NCERT.

Awasthi, V. (1989). *Developing Training Strategy for Science Teaching by Using Concept Attainment Model.* Ph.D. Education, Indore: Devi Ahalya Vishwa Vidyalaya.

Aziz, T. (1990). *A Study of the Comparative Effectiveness of the Information Processing Models of Teaching in Developing Certain Concepts in Chemistry at the Secondary Stage.* Ph.D. Education, New Delhi: Jamia Millia Islamia.

Badgley, R.E. (1956). *A General Studies Curriculum in Science and Mathematics for College of Education in Oregon.* Doctoral Dissertation, Colorado: University of Colorado.

Bandyopadhyay, J. (1984). *Environmental Influence, Academic Achievement and Scientific Aptitude as Determinants of Adolescents Attitude towards Science Stream.* Ph.D. Psychology, Calcutta: Calcutta University.

Barman, S. (1983). *The Origin and Development of Modern Science in Pre-Independence India.* Ph.D. History, Guwahati: Guwahati University.

Behera, D.K. (1981). *Evaluation to Text Book in Science.* M.Ed. Dissertation, Jyoti Vihar: Sambalpur University.

Behera, K.C. (1992). *Evaluation of Physical Science Text Book for Class IX prescribed by Board of Secondary Education, Orissa.* M.Ed. Dissertation, Jyoti Vihar: Sambalpur University.

Buch, M.B. et al. (1960). *Second Survey of Educational Research (1972-78).* New Delhi: S. Chand & Co. Ltd.

Buch, M.B. et al. (1997). *Fifth Survey of Educational Research (1988-92). Vol-I.* New Delhi: NCERT.

Bullington, A. (1949). *A Study of Science for General Education at the College Level.* Science Education 33:235-41.

Bullington, A. (1952). *The Subject Matters Content of General Education Science Course.* Science Education 36:285-92.

Dash, M. (1983). *An Analysis on Attitude of Girl Students towards Science and their Achievement at the Secondary Stage of Jharsuguda Town.* M.Ed. Dissertation, Jyoti Vihar: Sambalpur University.

Davis, D.D. (1962). *A Critical Analysis of the Students of Existing Biology Programmes in Texas Junior Colleges Compared with Established Objectives for the Biology Programme in Colleges of the United States.* Doctoral Dissertation, Texas: University of Texas.

Deshmukh, A.L. (1991). *Science Education as a Means of Social Change with Special Respect to Health and Hygenic Habits.* Ph.D. Education, Pune: Adarsha Comprehensive College of Education.

Dubey, K.K. (1992). *A Study of the Scientific Temper and its Measurement.* Ph.D. Education, Jabalpur: Rani Durgabai Viswavidyalaya.

Gagne, R.M. (1966). *Elementary Science ANCW Scheme of Instruction.* Science 151:49-53.

Ganguli, D. & Vashistha, U.C. (1991). *Research in Science Education: A Trend Report on Buch, M.B. (1991). Fourth Survey of Research in Education.* New Delhi: NCERT.

Ghosh, S. (1989). *A Critical Study of Scientific Attitude and Aptitude of the Students and Determination of Some Determinants of Scientific Attitude.* Ph.D. Education, Kalyani: University of Kalyani.

Goel, V.P. and Agbebi, E.A. (1990). *Learning Physics through Lecture Demonstration Method (LDM) and Individualised Instruction Method (IIM):* Indian Educational Review. Vol. 25(4), 84-89.

Gisler, J.R. (1967). *Science Up Grading at the High School Level.* The Progress of Education. November, 1967.

Good, C.V., Barr, A.S. & Scates, D.E. (1941). *Methodology of Educational Research.* New York.: Mapleton Century Craft.

Goyal, K.M. (1982). *In Buch, M.B. (1997). Fifth Survey of Educational Research (1988-92).* New Delhi: NCERT.

Gupta, S.P. (1969). *School Improvement Through Curriculum Development.* Teacher Education, Vol. III, No. 3, April.

Gurumurthy, C. (1990). *A Comparative Study of the Effectiveness of Guided Discovery Approach of doing Physics Experiments* versus *Instructed Performance Approach at Pre-University Level.* Ph.D. Education, Mysore: University of Mysore.

Hall, T.S. et al. (1961). *Science Teaching in Elementary and Junior High Schools.* Science Education. 133 : 2019-24.

Helgeson, S., Blosser, P.E. and Howe, R.W. (1977). *The Status of the Pre-College Science, Mathematics & Social Science Education: 1955-1975.* Science Education Vol-I, Columbus: Ohio State University.

Hernandez, D.F. (1960). *Developing Needs of Science Education in the Republic of the Philippines.* Doctoral Dissertation, Philadelphia: Indiana University.

Haque, S.S. (1987). *Open Book Test Examination in Class IX in General Science.* M.Ed. Dissertation, Jyoti Vihar: Sambalpur University.

Jena, B. (1982). *An Investigation into the Problems of Science Teachers Serving in the High Schools Situated in the District of Moyurbhanj.* M.Ed. Dissertation, Jyoti Vihar: Sambalpur University.

Jha, V. (1970). *An Investigation into some Factors Related to Achievement in Science on Secondary Schools Physical Education.* Patna: Patna University.

Kayathri, U.S. (1989). *An Investigation into the Effectiveness of Jerry Luca's Memory Model in Learning Botany.* M.Phil. Education, Karaikudi: Alagappa University.

Kelkar, S.A. (1950). *Tentative Course of Study in General Science.* Ph.D. Education, Bombay: Bombay University.

Khalid, A.M. (1954). *Science Education in the Iraqi Society.* Doctoral Dissertation, Columbia: Columbia University.

Khalwania, N.S. (1986). *Effectiveness of Concept-Based Science Curriculum in Developing Cognitive Structure and Acquisition of Process Skills Among High School Students.* Ph.D. Education, Patna: Patna University.

Krishnan, K.A. (1981). *A Critical Comprehensive Study of the Secondary School Science Curricula of Kerala and Tamilnadu.* Ph.D. Education, Thiruvananthapuram: Kerala University.

Kumar, U.S. (1991). *The Teaching of General Science and the Development of Scientific Attitude in Secondary School Students in Relation to Achievement in General Science.* M.Phil. Education, Annamalainagar: Annamalai University

Lambhate, M.V. (1987). *Development of Instructional Material for Teachers Teaching Science to Class VI in Rural Areas of MP.* Ph.D. Education, Indore: Devi Ahalya Vishwa Vidyalaya.

Malhotra, V.K. (1988). *A Critical Study of the Existing Facilities of Science Teaching and Construction of Evaluation Instruments for its Supervision in Different Types of Secondary Schools in Delhi.* Ph.D. Education, Delhi: University of Delhi.

Mandlia, S.S. (1988). *Attitudes of Secondary Stage Students Towards Science Curriculum and its Relationship with Achievement Motivation.* Ph.D. Education, Jaipur: University of Rajasthan.

Mehna, V.H. (1986). *An Investigation into Some Factors Affecting Academic Achievement in Science at Standard IX Students of Greater Bombay.* Ph.D. Education, Bombay: Bombay University.

Menon, S.S. (1986). *In Buch, M.B. (1997). Fifth Survey of Educational Research (1988-92).* New Delhi: NCERT.

Mishra, S. (1977). *A Sample Study of the Efficacy of Enquiry Teaching for Developing Scientific Concepts over Traditional Methods of Teaching Science,* M.Ed. Dissertation, Jyoti Vihar: Sambalpur University.

Mishra, K.A. (1980). *Study of Curricular Validity and Reliability of Examination in General Science Conducted by Board of Secondary Education, Orissa at Secondary Stage.* M.Ed. Dissertation, Jyoti Vihar: Sambalpur University.

Mishra, S. (1985). *Analysis of the Attitude of the Secondary School Children Towards Science.* M.Ed. Dissertation, Jyoti Vihar: Sambalpur University.

Mishra, K. (1987). *A Comparative Study of the Effectiveness of Two Different Types of Parallel Objective Achievement Test in General Science for Class VI.* M.Ed. Dissertation, Jyoti Vihar: Sambalpur University.

Mishra, R. (1990). *A Critical Appraisal of Teaching Science in Secondary Schools of Sambalpur District.* M.Ed. Dissertation, Jyoti Vihar: Sambalpur University.

Mohanty, B. (2001). *School Administration and Supervision,* New Delhi: Deep & Deep Publications Pvt. Ltd.

Mohanty, B., Mohanty, J. (2002). *Early Childhood Care and Education (ECCE),* New Delhi: Deep & Deep Publications Pvt. Ltd.

Mohanty, J. (2002). *Adult and Non-Formal Education (2nd Inlarged Edn.),* New Delhi: Deep & Deep Publications Pvt. Ltd.

Mohanty, J. (2003). *Teacher Education,* New Delhi: Deep & Deep Publications Pvt. Ltd.

Mohanty, J. (2003). *Education Technology,* New Delhi: Deep & Deep Publications Pvt. Ltd.

Mohanty, S. (2003). *Teaching of Science in Secondary Schools,* New Delhi: Deep & Deep Publications Pvt. Ltd.

Mohanty, S. (1987). *An Appraisal of Teaching Science in the High Schools of Cuttack City.* Ph.D. Education, Bhubaneswar: Utkal University.

Mohapatra, B.C. (1995). *Development of Software Package for Teaching Chemistry to Class IX Students of Madhya Pradesh State.* Ph.D. Education, Indore: Devi Ahalya Vishwa Vidyalaya.

Moore, M.R. (1965). *A Survey of College Biology Departments Regarding Introductory Courses Curricula and Advanced Placement Practices.* Journal of Research in Science Teaching, 3:235-45.

Muttaque, I.A. (1981). *Development of a Curriculum in Biology for Secondary Schools of Bangladesh.* Ph.D. Education, Baroda: M.S. University, Baroda.

Naik, N. (1993). *Science Teaching Facilities in Secondary Schools: A Case Study of Subarnapur.* M.Ed. Dissertation, Jyoti Vihar: Sambalpur University.

National Policy on Education (1986). Government of India, New Delhi: Ministry of Human Resource Development, Department of Education.

National Curriculum for Primary and Secondary Education: A Framework. (1985). pp. 1-14, New Delhi: NCERT.

Nayar, P. (1971). *Some Predictors of Achievements in Science at the Secondary School Stage.* Ph.D. Education, Trivandrum: Kerala University.

Padhi, J.S. (1993). *The Home: Effects on Pupil Academic Self-Concept and Achievement in Science.* Research Bulletin–Maharastra State Council of Educational Research and Training-23 (182) 4-8.

Patole, N.K. (1967). *A Study of Teaching of Science in Rural Primary Schools Standard I to VII.* Ph.D. Education, Pune: Poona University.

Patwardhan, S.S. (1995). *A Critical Study of the Difficulties and Mistakes in Marathi Writing by the Students of Standard VI of Bombay Municipal Corporation School and Effectiveness of*

Remedial Teaching and Learning Programme. Ph.D. Education, Mumbai: Shreemati Nathibai Damodar Thackere Women's University.

Pawar, S.S. (2004). *University Grants Commission (UGC) and Development of Libraries*, New Delhi: Deep & Deep Publications Pvt. Ltd.

Prabhat, R.K. and Singh, V. (1993). *Relationship between Ego Strength and Job Satisfaction*. Indian Journal of Psychology and Education, Vol. 24 (2) 99-102.

Pradhan, B. (1978). *An Analysis of the National Text-Book in Science (Physics) used in High School Classes IX, X, XI of Orissa*. M.Ed. Dissertation, Jyoti Vihar: Sambalpur University.

Rali, S. (1995). *A Study of the Awareness and Attitude of Teachers and Students of High Schools towards Environmental Education in Jabalpur District*. Ph.D. Education, Jabalpur: Rani Durgabai Viswavidalaya.

Ramdas, J. (1981). *Curriculum Development Science Relevant to the Indian School System*. Ph.D. Psychology, Pune: Poona University.

Ramesh, (1984). *In Buch, M.B. (1997). Fifth Survey of Educational Research (1988-92)*, New Delhi: NCERT.

Rao, G.K. (1995). *Study of Teachers Effectiveness in Relation to Creativity and Interpersonal Relationships*. Ph.D. Education, Waltier: Andhra University.

Revised National Policy on Education (1992). Government of India, New Delhi: Ministry of Human Resource Development, Department of Education.

Rout, R.C. (1982). *A Study of Relationship between Instruction and Achievement in General Science in the High Schools of Sambalpur Town*. M.Ed. Dissertation, Jyoti Vihar: Sambalpur University.

Rowe, M.B. (1969). *'Science and Soul'*. The Urban Review, No. 4 2:3 31-33.

Rup Prakash, (1968). *In Buch, M.B. (1979). Second Survey of Research in Education (1972-78)*. New Delhi: S. Chand & Co. Ltd.

Sangulang, L.E. (1961). *Some Aspects of Science Education for Rural Philippines and Implications for the Education of Teachers for the Community Schools*. Doctoral Dissertation, Philadelphia: Indiana University.

Sansanwal, D.N and Suri, S. (1995). *Comparative Effectiveness of Lecture Method Programmed Learning Material in Terms of*

Achievement in Organic Chemistry of Class XI Students. Experiments in Education, Vol. XXIII (2) 23-32, Indian Educational Abstracts, 3 July, 1997.

Sarangi, R.C. (1983). *A Study of Science Education in Orissa—A Comprehensive Analysis.* Ph.D. Education, Patna: Patna University.

SCERT, Andhra Pradesh (1980). *Evaluation Study of Text Books in Environmental Studies of Class III & V Based on Revised Curriculum in Science.* Hyderabad: Government of Andhra Pradesh.

Sharma, R. (1988). *In Modern Science Teaching.* New Delhi: Dhanpat Rai & Sons.

Sharma, M. and Parik, M. (1997). *A Study of Administrative Academic and Personal Problems, as Faced by Principals, Teachers and the Students of Navodaya Vidyalayas of Rajasthan.* Independent Study of Rajasthan, Indian Educational Abstracts-2, January.

Sharma, H.L. (1984). *A Critical Study of the Development of School Science Education in India from 1947 to 1977.* Ph.D. Education, New Delhi: Jamia Milia Islamia.

Sharma, R.D. (1995). *Influence of Recent Life Experience on Mental Health of School Teachers.* Indian Educational Review.

Sheth, U. (1967). *Construction and Stardardisation of Achievement Test in General Science for Standards V, VI and VII for Children Studying Through Gujarati as the Medium of Instruction in Greater Bombay.* Bombay: Bombay University.

Singh, V.S. (1977). *Development of a Curriculum in Science for Secondary Schools in the State of Maharastra.* Ph.D. Education, Bombay: Bombay University.

Singh, R.S. (1993). *Teacher Effectiveness in Relation their Sex, Area and Adjustment.* Bharatiya Shiksha Shodh Partrika. 12(2) 17-21.

Stake, R.E. and Easley, J.A. (1978). *Case Studies in Science Education,* Illinois: Urban University of Illinois Centre for Instructional Research and Curriculum Evaluation.

Sonar, M.S. (1975). *An Analytical Study of the Use of Filmstrips in Teaching of Science.* Ph.D. Education, Srinagar: Srinagar University.

Sood, J.K. (1992). *The Public Understanding of Science.* Independent Study. Ajmer: Ajmer Regional College of Education.

Thakur, D. and Thakur, D.N. (2004). *Vocational and Technical Education (2nd Edition)*, Deep & Deep Publications Pvt. Ltd., New Delhi.

Thampurthy, N.R. and Devi, G. (1994). *Introduction Effect of Creativity Attitude Towards Problem Solving and Social Position on the Achievement in Mathematics of Secondary School Pupils.* Ph.D. Education, Calcutta: University of Calcutta.

The Education Commission (1964-66). *Education and National Development.* New Delhi: Ministry of Education, Government of India.

The Secondary Education Commission (1952-53). New Delhi, Government of India, P. 77.

Tripathy, A.K. (1986). *Science Teaching Facilities in Secondary Schools. A Case Study of Bargarh Sub-division.* M.Ed. Dissertation, Jyoti Vihar: Sambalpur University.

Vaidya, N. (1989). *The Impact of Science Teaching.* New Delhi: Oxford & IBH Publishing Company.

Vaidya, N. (1997). *Science Education. Fifth Survey of Educational Research (1988-92).* Vol. I. New Delhi: NCERT.

Vaidya, N. (1998). *How to Build-up Conceptual Powers of Students,* New Delhi: Deep & Deep Publications Pvt. Ltd.

Vaidya, N. (1998). *How to Think Scientifically,* New Delhi: Deep & Deep Publications Pvt. Ltd.

Vaidya, N. (2003). *Science Teaching for the 21st Century,* New Delhi: Deep & Deep Publications Pvt. Ltd.

Vaidya, N. and Vaidya, S. (2002). *Encyclopaedia of Educational Foundations and Development (Set in 2 vols.),* New Delhi: Deep & Deep Publications Pvt. Ltd.

Vashistha, U.C. (1986). *In Buch, M.B. (1997). Fifth Survey of Educational Research (1988-92).* New Delhi: NCERT.

Veerappa, N.S. (1958). *In Buch, M.B. et al. (1991). Fourth Survey of Research in Education (1983-88).* Vol-I. New Delhi: NCERT.

Watson. F.G. (1963). *Research on Teaching Science.* In Gage N.L. (Ed) Handbook of Research on Teaching Rand. M.C. Nally PP. 1031-59.

Weiss, I.R. (1978). *Report of the 1977 National Survey of Science, Mathematics and Social Studies Education.* In Raleigh, N.C. Centre for Educational Research and Evaluation, Triangle Institute.

Woodburn, J.H., and Obourn, E.S. (1965). *Teaching the Pursuit of Science.* London: MacMillan, p. 470.

Index